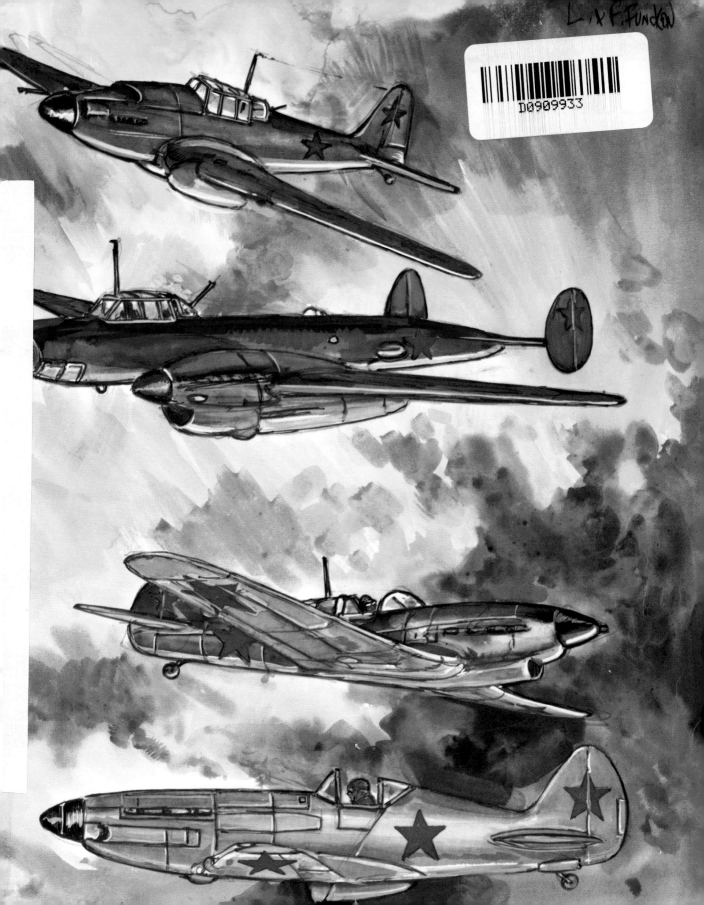

THE SECOND WORLD WAR

PART 2
Great Britain, Germany, France, USSR and Belgium, 1939-43

Liliane and Fred Funcken

Prentice-Hall, Inc., Englewood Cliffs, N.J.

SC RH

Contents

PART ONE: Great Britain

The Guards   6

Facing the Enemy Alone   10

The Regular Army   16

British Armoured Vehicles   20

The Royal Air Force   27

PART TWO: Armoured Vehicles and Aircraft

Russian Armoured Vehicles   38

Belgian Armoured Vehicles   44

The French Air Force   46

The German Air Force, 1939-41   52

The Soviet Air Force   62

The Belgian Air Force   66

PART THREE: Germany

The German Army, 1941-43   70

The Todt Organisation
and the Women's Services   80

The Afrika Korps   82

The Parachute Forces   84

The Russian Volunteers   88

The Waffen SS   92

Self-Propelled Guns   104

German Armoured Vehicles, 1941-43   106

The Luftwaffe, 1941-43   114

c. 1

Foreword

In the first of this series of four volumes devoted to the Second World War we explained why we had departed from following a strict chronology. We preferred instead to present to the reader a coherent picture within each book, rather than deal with each of the combatants at the point they entered the war, or divide the forces of the main nations into too many separate sections.

It would be impossible in the second of our volumes not to continue the fascinating story of the development of the German army, and we wanted also to devote a major part to the British army, which stood alone against the enemy in the dark days of 1940.

The fortunes of the war in the first years were determined by the resistance to the German *Blitzkrieg*, which brought into play the armoured divisions of the Allies, and the confrontation in the air of the RAF and the Luftwaffe. We have therefore also brought together in this volume the uniforms and arms of the men engaged in these heroic struggles.

We would like to offer our warmest thanks to:

The conservateurs of the Musée royal de l'Armée de Bruxelles—particularly Monsieur J. Lorette of the Cabinet des estampes—and Monsieur François T'Sas, in charge of research,

Monsieur M. Boulin, Conservateur, Musée international des Hussards de Tarbes,

Herr G. Dirrheimer, Assistant Keeper, Heeresgeschichtliches Museum, Vienna,

The Keeper of the Historical Institute of the Finnish armies and Lieutenant-Colonel Palmen,

Colonel E. Grimaldi, National Museum, Oslo,

Messieurs J. Borsarello and M. Landry, and also M. R. Guillaume, whose friendly help has been invaluable.

PART ONE

GREAT BRITAIN

The Guards

Of all the nations in the world Great Britain has the most splendid array of regiments, endowed with uniforms of dazzling colours. Among these, the most famous and representative are the regiments of the Household Brigade, which are entrusted with the privileged task of guarding the person of the Sovereign, without being exempt from the dangers of war when the occasion demands. Contrary to the opinion of some laymen, these 'parade-ground soldiers' have fought with outstanding valour on most battlefields since the reign of King Charles II, under which monarch the Household Brigade was first organised in 1660.

At this date the three first regiments comprising the King's personal bodyguard were the Life Guards, the Grenadier Guards and the Coldstream Guards. The Scots Guards were to join them in 1686, the Royal Horse Guards in 1820, the Irish Guards in 1900 and, finally, the Welsh Guards in 1915.

THE FOOT GUARDS

The Grenadier Guards

Originally called the 'Royal Regiment of Guards', the Grenadier Guards trace their history back to Lord Wentworth's Regiment, which fought so bravely at Dunkirk in 1658 when Charles II was in exile.

The Coldstream Guards

The Coldstream Guards began as a regiment in Cromwell's Parliamentary 'New Model Army', their original commander being George Monck, a former Royalist officer who had served the late King Charles I. Turning against his new masters, Monck gathered his troops together in a small Berwickshire village called Coldstream, on the border between England and Scotland, and from this time on (1659), the nickname of 'Coldstreamers' was given to dissident troops. It was the part played by Monck's soldiers in the Restoration of Charles II which led to them becoming the second regiment of Royal Foot Guards.

The Scots Guards

Descended from the troops raised by the 1st Marquess of Argyll in 1642 to serve King Charles I, this regiment was formed around a nucleus of survivors of 'His Majestie's Foote Regiment of his Lyffe Guard' of Charles II, defeated at the Battle of Dunbar in 1650. It took the Monmouth Rebellion of 1685 for the young regiment to be added to the Guards brigade the following year, the Scots Guards thereby earning the nickname of 'The Kiddies'.

GREAT BRITAIN, CEREMONIAL UNIFORMS

1. Trooper of the Royal Horse Guards (The Blues) — 2. Trooper of the Life Guards, dismounted duty, without breastplate (Both regiments form part of the Household Brigade.) — 3. Welsh Guards — 4. Officer of the Royal Scots — 5. Officer of the 9th Queen's Royal Lancers — 6–7. NCO (Sergeant) and Drummer, Royal Marines — 8. Grenadier Guards — 9. Coldstream Guards — 10. Scots Guards (no bearskin plume) — 11. Irish Guards

These three regiments, the Grenadier, the Coldstream and the Scots Guards, had the privilege of being the first to carry the costly but modern 'fusils', and they fought together for the first time at the Battle of Sedgemoor in 1685, a battle which put a stop to the exploits of the Duke of Monmouth. Together with the two older regiments, the Scottish regiment, now integrated into the Brigade of Guards, took the field against France from 1689 to 1697.

Three years later, the War of the Spanish Succession took the Royal Guards regiments back to the Continent along with an imposing British force. The Battles of Blenheim, Ramillies and Malplaquet took place, and in 1704, 1705 and 1727 there were also the tough struggles for the defence of Gibraltar. After a brief respite, the War of the Austrian Succession blazed up, during which the brigade saw action at the Battle of Dettingen in 1743. Two years later came the Battle of Fontenoy. Continually called upon, the Foot Guards took part in the Seven Years War and fought against the 'rebels' in the American War of Independence. Then it was France again, where the brigade won the right to embroider its first battle honour on its Colours: 'Lincelles'. But it would soon become tedious if we continued this impressive list: let us therefore leap forward through history, passing quickly over the campaigns of the Napoleonic wars and those in the Crimea, Egypt and South Africa, to mention the Battles of Mons, Le Cateau, Messines, Ypres, Arras and Cambrai during the First World War. The conflict with which we are particularly occupied in these pages shows no break in this extraordinary honours list. From 1939 the Household Brigade was present at least in part from Egypt to Norway and from Dunkirk to Algiers. The battle honours awarded to the Guards during those terrible years include the familiar names of El Alamein, Salerno, Anzio, Monte Cassino and Brussels.

Meanwhile, the ranks of the Household Brigade had been opened to other regiments and we must again go back a long way in time to look at the royal cavalry regiments, whose members had a history as distinguished as their comrades in the Foot Guards.

THE HOUSEHOLD CAVALRY

The Household Cavalry, which together with the regiments of Foot Guards makes up the Household Brigade, also traces its origins back to the sudden changes of fortune which accompanied Charles II's period in exile and his subsequent restoration.

The Life Guards

Until 1820 the Life Guards alone comprised the Household Cavalry. They first appeared in England with the return of Charles II and were then often called 'Horse Guards', a fact which adds to the problems of historians studying subsequent centuries.

In 1788 the Life Guards were divided into two regiments, these being amalgamated in 1922 into the present single regiment, which, in order of precedence, is the very first of all the regiments of the British army.

The Royal Horse Guards

Now nicknamed 'The Blues', because of the colour of their tunics, these cavalrymen made their appearance in 1661 as 'The Royal Regiment of Horse', although they were already familiarly known as 'The Oxford Blues'.

The title of 'Royal Regiment of Horse Guards' was granted to them in 1687 and helped to cause the confusion mentioned above. It was not until

GREAT BRITAIN, KHAKI UNIFORMS AND BATTLE DRESS

1–2. Field service dress and equipment, front and back — 3. Walking-out dress, with field service cap — 4. Field service dress and equipment, with greatcoat — 5. Belgian volunteer in Britain — 6. Military policeman (guard for strategic points in Britain) — 7–8. Field service dress in Libya — 9. Officer of a South African Scottish regiment in service dress — 10. Officer of the Scots Guards in service dress. Note the special Guards cap with the peak lying flat over the forehead, obliging the wearer to keep his head erect; also the arrangement of the buttons in accordance with the pattern peculiar to each Guards regiment (here in groups of three), and the plus-fours, introduced into British military fashion by the Foot Guards — 11–12. Regulation field service cap, as it was normally worn, and unfolded for winter wear. However, it was rarely worn in this way and was dropped in 1943.

1820 that the Blues were incorporated into the Household Cavalry. This belated honour did not, however, prevent the Life Guards and the Royal Horse Guards from performing well together on the battlefields, but the campaigns at the beginning of the eighteenth century were fought without them and the Blues had to wait until 1748 before seeing action in Flanders and then throughout the Seven Years War. The two regiments were to be awarded many honours during the Napoleonic Wars, fighting side by side in Spain as well as at Waterloo. During the Second World War the Household Cavalry was formed into armoured regiments which were to fight magnificently in North Africa and Italy, as well as in the north-west Europe campaign from Normandy until the final operations in Germany.

This reminder of more recent campaigns has taken us a long way from the time when officers bore their old Civil War rank and their new Guards rank simultaneously. Officers could then purchase their commissions, from the highest rank to the most junior, although there were strict rules designed to prevent the entry of the wealthy but incompetent. This highly undemocratic practice persisted until the middle of the nineteenth century.

UNIFORMS

It was in 1840 that the soldiers of the Household Brigade began to wear the uniform which, apart from a few minor modifications, we admire so much today. The forerunner of the present cavalry helmet was introduced in 1842; two years earlier the famous bearskin cap had been worn for the first time by the Foot Guards. The tunic was not adopted until 1855 and it was only in 1872 that the Foot Guards first wore the complete uniform which is still worn.

It may be noted here that among the regiments not belonging to the Household Brigade there are many still in existence which are able to pride themselves upon an equally long and distinguished history.

Facing the Enemy Alone

In July 1940, following the disastrous campaign on the Continent and the brilliant strategic success of the withdrawal from Dunkirk—achieved thanks to the sacrifice of thirty thousand French soldiers—Great Britain found herself alone against the formidable and seemingly invincible German forces. Of the troops comprising the British Expeditionary Force, a quarter had been lost, as had all their equipment: the number of trained soldiers immediately available now totalled 325,000 men. The situation regarding equipment was even more catastrophic: only five hundred guns, fifty infantry tanks and two hundred light tanks could be put into the field. There remained, of course, the famous and all-powerful Royal Navy and also the less than all-powerful Royal Air Force with its five to six hundred fighters—most of which were obsolescent—and some five hundred bombers.

This disturbing military weakness can be easily explained. Since the First World War, powerful currents of popular opinion had been against any future intervention in a European conflict. As a result, the funds allocated to arms production had been strictly limited and the armed forces had been forced to rely on voluntary enlistment. After the fruitless meetings between Chamberlain and Hitler at Munich, however, Britain had begun to strengthen her slender Territorial divisions, bringing them up to thirteen in number. To do this, compulsory military service was introduced in peacetime, a unique

BRITISH INFANTRY WEAPONS

1. ·303 No. 1 Mark III rifle — 2. ·303 No.4 Mark I rifle — 3. ·303 P 14 rifle, subsequently designated the No.3 Mark I rifle in 1939 — 4. 9 mm Sten Mark I sub-machine gun — 5. 9 mm Sten Mark II — 6. 9 mm Sten Mark III — 7. 9 mm Sten Mark IV — 8. ·455 Thompson Model 1928 sub-machine gun, developed from the Model 1921 known as the 'Tommy Gun' or 'Chicago Piano', made famous by the gangsters during the Prohibition — 9. ·455 Webley No. 1 Mark IV revolver — 10. ·455 Webley automatic pistol — 11. Soldier firing the Bren gun (automatic rifle) — 12. ·303 Vickers Medium machine gun — 13. Mills grenade — 14. 7·7 mm Bren gun (automatic rifle). This weapon could be mounted on a tripod. It was occasionally used as an anti-aircraft weapon, but was very quickly abandoned for this purpose because of the wastage of ammunition.

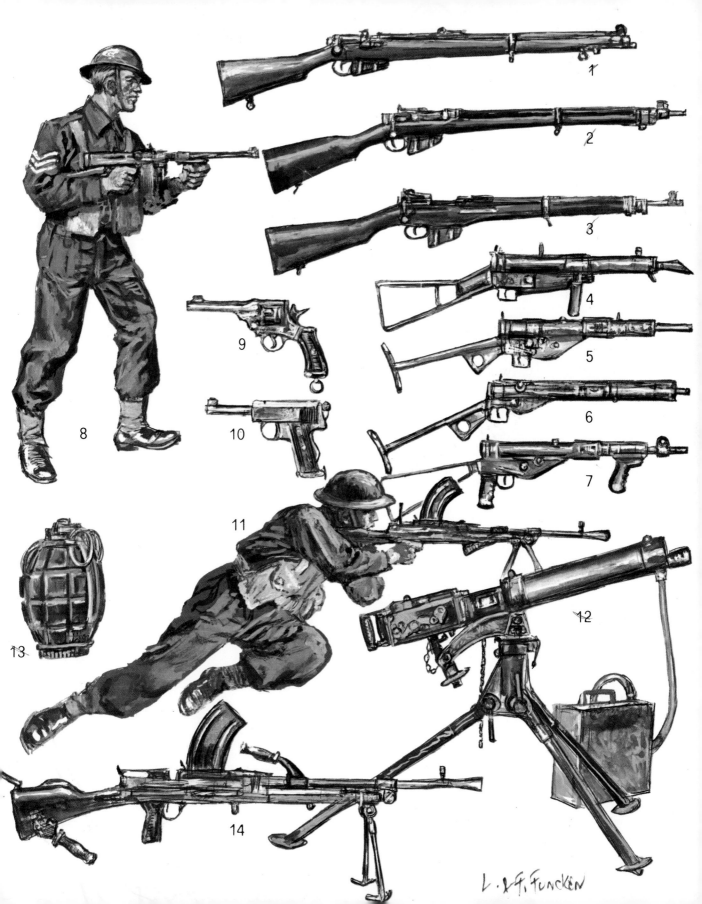

occurrence in the history of the British people, but military manpower was thereby doubled. Nevertheless, intervention on the Continent had to be on a modest scale : thirteen divisions, of which three were Territorial formations. After Dunkirk, the British Army had just one intact division worthy of the name.

It now became a matter of real urgency to reorganise and reequip the survivors of the British Expeditionary Force (BEF) of which, happily, there were many. The government also appealed to Canada and the United States, who provided Britain with considerable quantities of the weapons needed for the reconstituted divisions. In this period too the nationals of the Allied countries who found themselves on British soil volunteered in large numbers for service in the British armed forces and an Act of Parliament passed on 31 August 1940 authorised the formation of six foreign armies which received into their ranks the volunteers of six nations : France, Belgium, Poland, Norway, Holland and Czechoslovakia.[1]

A considerable and decisive contribution was made by the Dominions, who spontaneously and energetically threw in their lot with the United Kingdom : 200,000 Canadians, 180,000 Australians, 190,000 New Zealanders and 120,000 South Africans, not to mention soldiers from other parts of the Empire, particularly India, were to see action on all fronts. It is as well to emphasise, however, that purely British forces fought everywhere alongside their Allies ; 70 per cent of the losses incurred between 1940 and 1941 were suffered by the British. In Tunisia, for instance, 90 per cent of the forces were British citizens.

THE HOME GUARD

After 19 July 1940, the date on which Hitler issued 'Instruction No. 16', which served as a prelude to the invasion of Great Britain by setting Operation *Seelöwe* (Sealion) in motion, the whole of the British people armed and prepared themselves for the defence of their island, particularly against attacks by the enemy's paratroops, who had achieved such unexpected results against the Belgians and Dutch a

1 These volunteer armies are discussed in vol. 4 of this series.

few months previously. There was neither terror nor panic, but instead an extraordinary determination in the citizens, who were obsessed with this threat from the skies and who were prepared to deal with it wherever it should occur. Throughout the British Isles, masses of volunteers began to search the skies and to erect barricades, most of which were improvised and were guarded by ferocious 'watch-dogs' armed with the most motley collection of weapons.

It was from these spontaneously organised militia units that the body of Local Defence Volunteers, subsequently called the Home Guard, was to emerge. All men between the ages of seventeen and sixty who were not in the armed forces were invited to enlist, the government undertaking to arm and equip them, although their services were without pay. By the evening of the first day, 250,000 such volunteers had joined up. From this moment on, it became increasingly difficult to clothe, let alone to arm, the ever-growing number of recruits. There were, for instance, only seventy thousand rifles immediately available, though a general collection brought in a further twenty thousand assorted firearms and an even larger number of weapons of older vintage, ranging from cutlasses to hunting spears.

Nevertheless, in spite of all these difficulties, the first regiments appeared in August 1940, to be attached to their respective county regiments. Bit by bit, weapons purchased from all corners of the world were distributed : principally automatic weapons intended to enable their bearers to fight more

BRITISH ANTI-INVASION WEAPONS AND TECHNIQUES

1. ·30 Garand semi-automatic rifle (USA) — 2. ·45 Thompson sub-machine gun or 'Squirtgun' — 3. 9 mm Star sub-machine gun (Spain) — 4. ·30 Johnson semi-automatic rifle (USA) — 5. ·30 Johnson automatic rifle (USA) — 6. 9 mm Astra automatic pistol (Spain). This weapon was unusual in being able to take nearly all types of 9 mm cartridges — 7. Road trap for troop-carrying aircraft. The aircraft lands on the road and (a) its undercarriage sinks into the specially-dug trench obstacle. (b) The aircraft tips up on to its nose and (c) turns over on to its back. — 8. Trench obstacles dug across potential landing-grounds — 9. Road obstacles, including tripod barriers and vehicles filled with stones or boulders. It should be remembered that these various traps were never put to the test as the invasion did not take place.

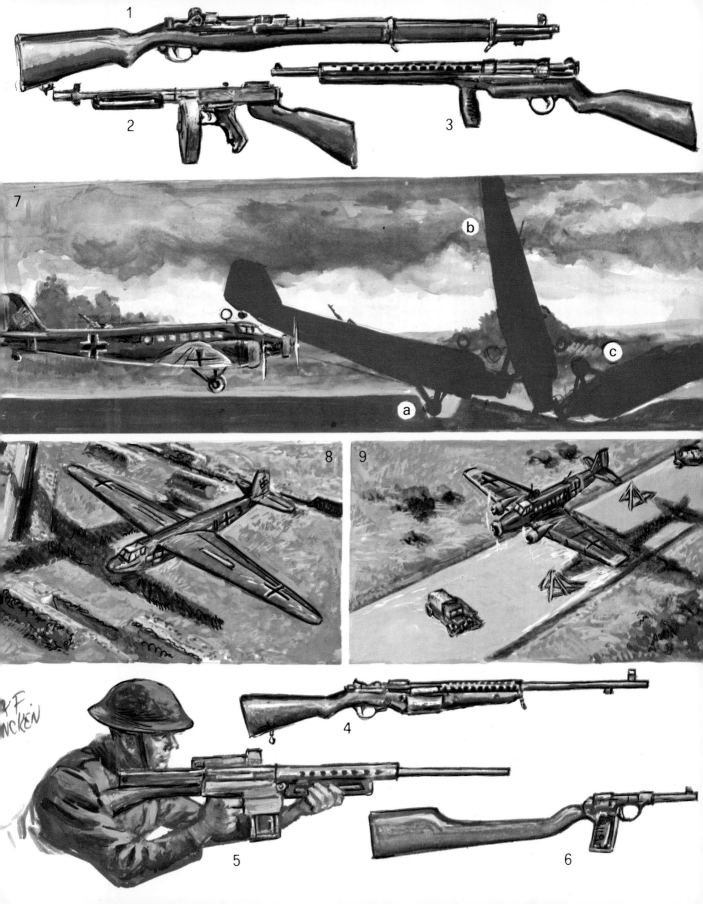

effectively against an enemy which had been widely equipped with them for a long time. Among those weapons which particularly attracted interest and attention were the Model 28 Thompson sub-machine gun, a weapon made famous by the American gangsters, which was of exceptionally high quality but very expensive; and the Spanish Astra Model 400 automatic pistol, which had the unusual distinction of being able to fire all types of 9 mm cartridge, including the Bergmann-Bayard, the Steyr, the Parabellum and the Browning.

Although the regular regiments were given priority in the distribution of these weapons (as well as a number of others reproduced here) the Home Guard too was eventually to be well provided with arms, even when it had achieved a strength of twelve hundred battalions, or one million men, by 1941. Compulsory service, which was introduced the same year, brought this imposing force up to a strength of 1,750,000 recruits, now officially called soldiers. By 1943 some two million men of the Home Guard, well-trained and of excellent morale, were able to perform innumerable tasks which would otherwise have tied down regular troops who were likely to be far more useful elsewhere.

In the field anti-invasion preparations were pushed forward with the greatest possible vigilance. Anti-tank ditches were everywhere, as were trenches designed to prevent German transport aircraft from landing anywhere in the country, while on the roads barricades were provided which could be erected in a short space of time. Any potential fifth column activity was quickly dealt with by the internment of German and Italian nationals in camps, which were not too uncomfortable. Place names on stations and on publicity signs and hoardings around towns were painted out, and even the most elementary but effective of all such measures—the pulling up of signposts—was not overlooked. All this was surely enough to confuse even the most astute parachutist.

In the increasingly unlikely event of an assault of this type actually happening, the attackers would have had several other nasty surprises to face, such as kiosks or information offices which were built of concrete and crammed with machine guns, the last resort of the British sense of humour!

Uniform

The uniform of the Home Guard was identical to that of the regular army. To start with there was no special insignia except for an armband with the letters HG. Later they used the sleeve insignia as illustrated on page 19.

THE WOMEN'S SERVICES

Of all the belligerent powers, Britain was the first to enlist women, although they were not made to carry arms. At most, such as in the case of wireless and searchlight operators with the anti-aircraft defences, they were authorised to 'help' their male companions to destroy the enemy. In 1941 170,000 women were engaged in this dangerous activity.

The biggest of all the women's formations was the QAIMNS or Queen Alexandra's Imperial Military Nursing Service, founded in 1881. Far behind came various other voluntary formations and organisations, including:

TANS or Territorial Army Nursing Service;
The VADs, comprising the SJAS, or Voluntary Aid Detachment of the St John Ambulance Society (1882), and the BRCS, or Voluntary Aid Detachment of the British Red Cross Society (1882);
ATS or Auxiliary Territorial Service (1938);
FANY or First Aid Nursing Yeomanry (1909);
NAAFI or Navy, Army and Air Force Institutes (1921).

BRITISH INFANTRY WEAPONS

1. Boys ·55 anti-tank rifle. Reputed to be totally ineffective and very unpopular, this weapon nevertheless proved formidable in the hands of crack soldiers on a few rare occasions — 2. 2-inch mortar — 3. Method of firing a 2-inch mortar — 4. 3-inch mortar — 5. 3-inch mortar and its crew — 6. Method of carrying and transporting the 3-inch mortar

In addition, the official auxiliary services were backed up by an impressive number of semi-military organisations, such as the Women's Auxiliary Service, Home Guard Auxiliaries, Mechanised Transport Corps, Auxiliary Fire Service, Women's Transport Service, Women's Land Army, etc.

The ATS, who were well known on the Continent, saw service on all fronts, and one hundred and twenty-seven of them lost their lives during the struggle. In spite of what many people may have thought, the Women's Services together won many citations and awards for bravery, one example being the Military Medal awarded to Sergeant Joan Mortimer of the WAAF (Women's Auxiliary Air Force). During a heavy raid on the RAF fighter station at Biggin Hill, on 18 August 1940, she calmly marked the unexploded bombs with the little red flags which she was carrying with her.

Uniforms

Several of the principal uniforms are shown in the illustrations. The only detail we shall add here is that, in the field, the ATS generally wore on the left breast the insignia of the regiment or corps to which they were attached. The forage cap was only worn with walking-out dress.

The Regular Army

UNIFORM

In 1937 a new-style uniform appeared, gradually replacing the First World War type which was still in service, though the old uniform was retained by certain regiments until 1940, particularly by the Guards, who arranged the buttons in the traditional manner appropriate to each regiment of Foot Guards. This new field service uniform, or battle dress as it was called, was not greeted with any overwhelming enthusiasm, for its austere and functional appearance had the disadvantage of making it look more like a boiler suit than a real uniform. However, it must be acknowledged that what it lost on an aesthetic level was largely counter-balanced by the fact that it was both practical and comfortable.

One irritating fact that disappointed even the untidiest of John Bull's soldiers was that, for security reasons, the battle dress could not bear any of the fine badges which had once so splendidly adorned even the coarsest khaki. However, a little later on, the authorities had to bow to the inevitable and accept the discreet introduction of small coloured strips bearing the name of the regiment. Gaudy cloth badges and formation signs soon followed, which broke down the comparative anonymity of the battle dress uniform even further.

The forage cap, or field service cap, although very elegant, was almost totally impractical. It did not offer adequate protection to the head in bad weather, it easily fell off, and it became quickly soiled by perspiration. Designed so that it could be pulled down over the neck and ears in cold weather, it then became a totally nondescript and rather depressing garment which brought to mind the Retreat from Moscow, and gave even the most fastidious soldier the appearance of a tramp at the end of his tether. Thus the field service cap disappeared one fine day to be replaced, in 1943, by the beret: looking strange enough on some

BRITISH WOMEN'S SERVICES

1. Auxiliary Territorial Service (ATS) — 2. Women's Royal Naval Service — 3. Women's Auxiliary Air Force — 4. Queen Alexandra's Imperial Military Nursing Service (QAIMNS) — 5. As above, in khaki service dress
Women's Royal Naval Service: 6. Cap badge — 7. Sleeve rank insignia of a director — 8. Superintendent — 9. Chief Officer — 10. Medical Superintendent — 11. First Officer — 12. Second Officer — 13. Third Officer
Auxiliary Territorial Service: 14. Cap badge — 15. Field service cap — 16. Shoulder strap rank insignia of a Chief Commander — 17. Senior Commander — 18. Junior Commander — 19. Subaltern — 20. Second Subaltern — 21. Badge worn by members of the Queen Alexandra's Imperial Military Nursing Service — 22. Shoulder strap worn by a Matron-in-chief of Queen Alexandra's Royal Naval Service — 23. Shoulder strap worn by a reserve nursing sister of the same service
Women's Auxiliary Air Force: 24. Sleeve rank insignia of a Squadron Officer — 25. Flight Officer — 26. Section Officer — 27. Assistant Section Officer

heads but having the advantage of being much more practical.

The introduction of the new headgear also provided the opportunity for clearer distinctions to be made between different arms of service. A khaki beret was worn by the infantry, black by armoured troops, red by airborne troops and green by Commandos.

EQUIPMENT

In 1937 the 1908-pattern cartridge-pouches came to the end of their long career, to be replaced by new large pouches, each of which could hold a string of canvas bags carrying ten 5-round magazines for the rifle or three 30-round magazines for the Bren gun; 32-round magazines for the Sten sub-machine gun could also be contained in these pouches when this new weapon was introduced in 1941.

WEAPONS

Rifles

Since 1939 the standard weapon of the British infantrymen had been the No. 4 Mark I rifle, which was a simplified version, for mass production, of the No. 1 Lee-Enfield of 1916. The long First World War bayonet was now judged to be too cumbersome, and one of the modifications to the new rifle was its adaptation to take a short bayonet, which looked, unfortunately, a little like a glorified nail and which was highly unpopular, as its appearance could hardly

be described as menacing. This retrograde step was doubly strange since the old bayonet had been designed to compensate for the comparatively limited length of the SMLE (Short Magazine Lee-Enfield). However, it is true that the First World War had proved that cold steel was only rarely used in modern conflicts.

This mass-produced No. 4 Mark I, then, armed the majority of British troops. Another version of this weapon was manufactured in North America (this is often confused with the original model, from which indeed it differed very little, even to the extent of bearing the same name). Five million units of this version alone were made. In addition to these 'twin' models, there were four other variants of the same Lee-Enfield in service. Of these, the No. 1 Mark III, which dated back to 1907, was still widely used, notably by the troops in the Middle East.

Apart from these purely British rifles, the shortage of weapons during the early months of the war led to the more or less temporary appearance of foreign rifles. Some of the principal models can be found in the illustrations.

Revolvers and Pistols

The most widely issued standard revolver was the Enfield No. 2 Mark I, adopted in 1932. This ·38 (9·65 mm) calibre weapon strongly resembled the Webley Mark IV, which was of the same calibre but much less common. The old ·455 calibre Webley No. 1 Mark IV, introduced in 1916, was also still in service. Adopted

GREAT BRITAIN, RANKS AND INSIGNIA

1 and 4. Field-Marshal — 2 and 5. General — 2 and 6. Lieutenant-General — 2 and 7. Major-General — 3 and 8. Brigadier. — 3 and 9. Colonel — 10. Lieutenant-Colonel — 11. Major — 12. Captain — 13. Lieutenant — 14. Second Lieutenant — 15. Conductor and Staff Sergeant-Major, 1st Class (rank not worn in the Household Cavalry and Foot Guards) — 16. Regimental Corporal-Major (Household Cavalry), Regimental Sergeant-Major (Foot Guards), Warrant Officer 1st Class in other regiments — 17. Regimental Quartermaster-Corporal (Household Cavalry), Regimental Quartermaster-Sergeant (Foot Guards), Quartermaster-Sergeant in other regiments — 18. Squadron Corporal-Major, Warrant Officer 2nd Class (Household Cavalry), Company Sergeant-Major (Foot Guards), Warrant Officer 2nd Class in other regiments — 19. Squadron Quartermaster and Corporal (Household Cavalry) — 20. Squadron or

Company Quartermaster — 21. Sergeant or Lance-Sergeant — 22. Corporal — 23. Lance-Corporal — 24. Corporal (Household Cavalry) — 25. Home Guard insignia — 26. Tradesman 1st Class, worn on the right sleeve (by Lance-Corporals and Privates only) — 27. Good conduct stripes (worn on the left sleeve) — 28. Gun Layer — 29. Layer of a light machine gun — 30. Badge of the Royal Scots Greys — 31. 9th Queen's Royal Lancers — 32. 17th/21st Lancers — 33. Royal Regiment of Artillery — 34. Royal Corps of Signals — 35. Royal Engineers — 36. Royal Army Medical Corps — 37. Grenadier Guards — 38. Scots Guards — 39. Welsh Guards — 40. Irish Guards — 41. Queen's Royal Regiment (West Surrey) — 42. The Buffs (Royal East Kent Regiment) — 43. South Wales Borderers — 44. The Royal Norfolk Regiment — 45. Seaforth Highlanders
'Pips' or stars, used to denote rank: 46. Grenadier, Coldstream and Welsh Guards — 47. Scots Guards — 48. Irish Guards — 49. Rifle Regiments and Chaplains

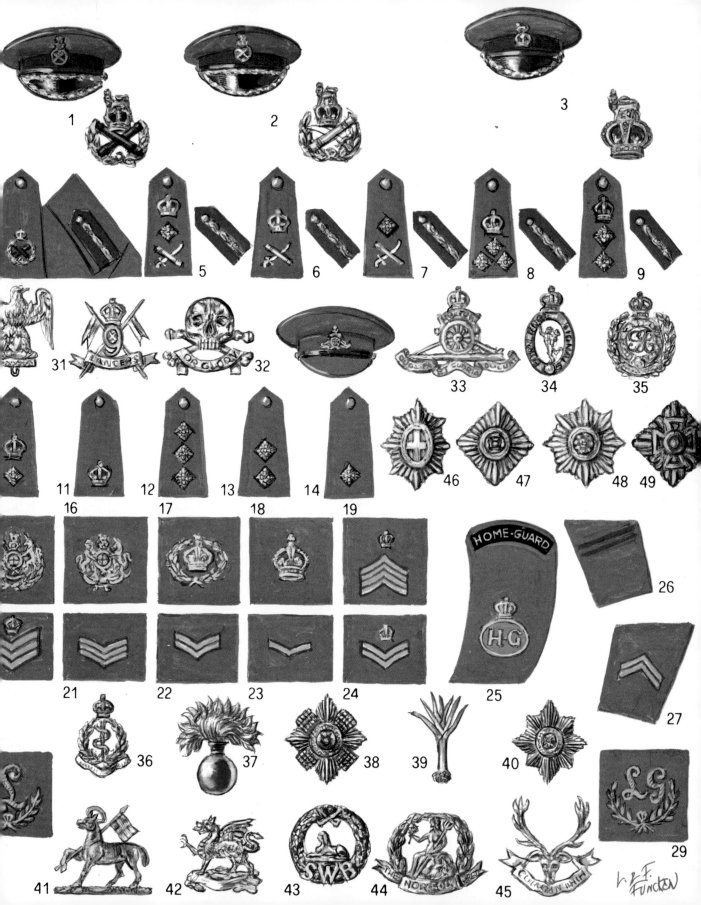

1   2   3

5   6   7   8   9

31   LANCERS   32   OR GLORY   33   34   35

11   12   13   14   46   47   48   49

16   17   18   19

21   22   23   24   HOME-GUARD   HG   26   25   27

36   37   38   39   40   29   LG

41   42   43   SWB   44   THE NORFOLK   45

in the light of the Colonial wars in which the need for powerful ammunition capable of stopping the most ferocious warriors had been strongly felt, this large calibre revolver nevertheless required a very experienced shot. The Webley automatic, of the same calibre, which had been issued to the navy in 1912, was used throughout the war.

Sub-Machine Guns

The sub-machine gun appeared in Great Britain in 1940, as we have indicated above, so that a more effective defence could be mounted against the expected invaders. These arms were all of foreign origin and only one of them, the ·45 calibre Thompson Model M1, adopted by the United States Army in 1942, remained in prolonged use.

The first purely British sub-machine gun was the Sten, the name of which had been created by taking the first letter of the surnames of each of its inventors, Shepperd and Turpin, and the first two letters of Enfield, where the Royal Small Arms Factory was located. This weapon was manufactured from 1941 onwards, in five different versions, of which the second or Mark II variant is by far the most celebrated. Mainly issued to the army and to Resistance units, the crudeness of its manufacture led people to remark that it could be made in any garage, and earned it such unflattering nicknames as 'Plumber's Delight' and the 'Stench Gun'. In spite of all this, the weapon performed its dreadful work just as efficiently as its more sophisticated counterparts.

The Bren Gun (or automatic rifle)

Adopted as the result of an open competition in 1925, the Bren owed its name to the Czechoslovakian town of Brno, the home of the Czech firm ZB, which won the £3,000 first prize. The first two letters of Brno, followed by the first two letters of Enfield, were used to form the name 'Bren'. Famed for its robustness, the Bren was most often used to fire single shots or short five-round bursts. When the fire was sustained at the rate of three thirty-round magazines a minute, the barrel overheated and had to be changed after the tenth magazine. Produced in 1937, this formidable 7·7 mm weapon proved itself one of the best of its kind.

The Machine Gun

This was the fine old Vickers model of 1912, based on the American Maxim system. Throughout the Second World World War it performed with the same unruffled steadfastness as it had in the First, to be replaced by a new model only recently.

British Armoured Vehicles

The bugle which sounded the Armistice on 11 November 1918 signalled also, at almost the same moment, the end of British tank production. Ironically, the country which had developed the first tank now on 12 November 1918, passed a law which drastically cut short her production of armoured fighting vehicles, a measure which was, however, necessitated by a very real need for economy. It was in this austere climate—and perhaps also as a result of it—that the revolutionary ideas of Captain B. H. Liddell Hart were born. As early as 1922 this remarkable military writer had described the armoured division of the future: it should include three hundred heavy and light tanks divided into battalions and forming, with motorised artillery battalions and infantry battalions transported in armoured vehicles, three mechanised brigades.

Liddell Hart was not the only advocate of armour. Even before him, General J.F.C. Fuller, former Chief of Staff of the Tank Corps, had made known his highly unorthodox views on the future role of the tank. He regarded the tank as a 'land cruiser', whose sole but decisive task was to make at full speed for its main

BRITISH ARMOURED VEHICLES I

1. Light Tank Mark VIB — 2. Cruiser Tank Mark I — 3. Cruiser Tank Mark II — 4. Cruiser Mark III — 5. Cruiser Mark IV — 6. Sleeve badge (worn on the upper arm), tank crews — 7. Tank driver's badge — 8. Cap badge of the Royal Tank Corps

1

6

7

8

2

3

4

5

strategic or tactical objective in order to disorganise the enemy command system. This concept of the fighting tank, following the example of the warship, had been put forward in 1916 by another 'rebel', Major G. le Q. Martel, who had entered the lists in his turn. Curbing their imagination, however, these two apostles of the cruiser tank had to reconcile themselves to a revision of their over-audacious ideas—which were in any case unrealisable within the technical limits of the period—and to concentrate on an excellent scheme for rapid and mobile armoured units. This desire for speed and mobility, which proved attractive to everyone, was achieved by the only means then possible—by producing small and lightly armoured vehicles which could avoid the fire of heavy weapons by virtue of their manoeuvrability. The opinion of the time leaned heavily in favour of a mass of light, cheaply produced tanks rather than a limited number of powerful but over-expensive tanks.

The first new tanks appeared in the 1920s. Although basically well designed, they could offer only very poor resistance to infantry weapons, and this troublesome weakness, which was barely remedied in later models, was to be harshly penalised in the first operations of the Second World War, showing that mobility by itself did not make up for inadequate protective armour. The tactical ideas of Liddell Hart were more or less put into practice, but in the unrealistic atmosphere of the 1920s completely erroneous conclusions had been drawn from manoeuvres which had little real meaning. The British prophets had in fact infinitely more success with a very gifted pupil by the name of Guderian, who was, unfortunately, a German.

Despite all these mistakes, however, it must be emphasised that the British tank had in fact made significant progress. G. le Q. Martel had designed and built, at his own expense, a small one-man tank which, after some very conclusive tests, served as the model for the production of a series of very interesting little machines known as 'tankettes'. The model developed by the firm of Carden-Loyd is particularly worthy of attention. The two founders of the form—Carden, the manager of a large garage, and John Loyd, his employer—were both excellent mechanics and this happy partnership quickly flourished, to achieve universal recognition when the two men became associated with the powerful Vickers-Armstrong company. Their tiny armoured vehicles gave rise to a whole new generation of 'tankettes', called 'Carriers', which appeared in 1936.

The most famous of these 'tankettes' was undoubtedly the Bren Gun Carrier, so named because it carried the famous automatic rifle (called a light machine gun in Britain). Then came the Cavalry Carrier and the Scout Carrier. Still more variants, such as the Mortar Carrier, were built—sometimes in vast numbers, as with the Universal Carrier, which reached the record production figure of thirty-five thousand for the United Kingdom alone; Canada, for her part, built twenty-nine thousand of them between 1941 and 1942.

The British armoured force, known as the 'Mechanised Force', owed an equal debt to Carden-Loyd for its first turreted tank in 1927, the Light Tank Mark I, which was to have a long line of descendants.

The disappointing experiments of 1927 and 1928 led not only to the abandonment of the concept of combined operations by tanks and other arms, but also, alas, to the continued predominance of the old and tenaciously held faith in large armoured units, to which infantry or artillery could be attached according to the circumstances. The first 'Tank Brigade' was formed in 1931, with four battalions of light and medium tanks. The cavalry was then

BRITISH ARMOURED VEHICLES II

1. Crusader I — 2. Crusader II — 3. Infantry Tank Mark I Matilda I — 4. 'Beaver' light armoured reconnaissance vehicle or scout car. This nickname had nothing to do with the animal but was chosen in honour of Lord Beaverbrook. — 5. Crossley armoured car — 6. Guy armoured car used by the Belgian volunteers in Great Britain

mechanised and its units grouped together in 1938 in the first 'Mobile Division', which was composed of the following:

1 tank brigade of three battalions;

2 mechanised cavalry brigades each containing three regiments, which, in reality, represented 3 battalions of light tanks;

2 artillery regiments;

2 motorised infantry regiments.

This was a long way from the lavish schemes of Liddell Hart!

A new Vickers tank, the A9 or Cruiser Tank Mark I, first saw the light of day in 1937; it was an appearance which marked the beginning of the quest for more powerful tanks. A version which was specially designed to act as an infantry tank when required was also put into production. This was the Cruiser Tank Mark II or A10, but it was badly received. After more than 125 examples of the A9 had been built, it was replaced by a superior model, the A13 or Cruiser Tank Mark III, which was in fact based on the revolutionary American tank conceived by that outstanding engineer, J. Walter Christie. The main advocate of the A13 was again the indefatigable G. le Q. Martel, by now a lieutenant-colonel. The immediate successor of the A13, the A15 or Cruiser Tank Mark VI—known as the 'Crusader'—came on to the scene too late to take part in the first battles on the Continent. It thus avoided being captured and was to achieve an infinitely more glorious destiny in Libya.

Several other models were produced by different companies throughout this period, such as the 'Matilda', developed at Woolwich Arsenal and made by the Vulcan Foundry Ltd. The small Mark I Matilda infantry tanks were to fight in some numbers alongside their big brothers, the Mark II Matildas, in France and North Africa. All bore the same nickname, although it was more generally applied to the Mark II version.

In 1939 the 'Mobile Division' became the 'Armoured Division', with two armoured brigades, one with three regiments of light tanks and the other equipped with heavy tanks of the cruiser type, comprising in all 108 light and 213 heavy tanks. This significant reduction in strength was, it was claimed, compensated for by the presence of the heavy tanks; but it now included only a single motorised infantry battalion and a single small artillery regiment. This relative weakness was remedied to some extent in 1940 by the addition of an extra motorised infantry regiment and a mixed anti-aircraft and anti-tank artillery regiment. At the same time, the 'Armoured Division' was split into two divisions of three armoured regiments each.

Following the disastrous campaign in France, the strength of these divisions was considerably reinforced by the addition of armoured reconnaissance vehicles and anti-tank and anti-aircraft artillery, the latter now better equipped with more powerful 40 mm weapons. In 1942 three armoured divisions could be put into the line. Reorganised the following year, each division lost an armoured brigade but in return was given a motorised infantry brigade. The number of tanks in each division fell to 188.

Although there were eleven British armoured divisions at one stage, the number had, incredibly, slipped back to five by the eve of the Normandy landings, the tanks of the six divisions which had been disbanded being used to swell the armoured units supporting the infantry. This strange reversal of policy was based upon what were considered to be fundamental differences between the operational conditions in North Africa and those likely to be experienced in Europe, where it was expected that the anti-tank defences could not be overcome by tanks alone. Armoured fighting vehicles were thereby declared unsuitable for anything other than the exploitation of results already achieved by the combined action of other arms.

The organisation of 1944-5 reverted to that of 1942, although the armoured car regiment was replaced by a regiment of reconnaissance tanks. The total number of tanks in each division now reached 365. The last models of the war will be illustrated and described in vol. 4.

BRITISH ARMOURED VEHICLES III

1. Infantry Tank Mark II Matilda II — 2. Valentine III (North Africa 1941) — 3. Churchill III (as used at Dieppe in 1942) — 4. Bren Carrier Mark I, 1940 — 5. Fordson armoured car

1

2

3

4

5

T 13269

L. & F. Funcken

SYNOPSIS OF THE PRINCIPAL BRITISH TANKS FROM 1939 TO 1942

TYPE	WEIGHT (TONS)	SPEED (mph)	RANGE[1] (miles)	ARMAMENT	CREW	PRODUCTION AND SERVICE
Vickers-Armstrong carriers						
Mark I Medium Machine gun Carrier	4	29·5	155	One Browning ·303-inch machine gun	3	
Mark I Bren Carrier	4	29·5	155	One 7·7 mm Bren gun	3	1,280 built in 1940; France in 1940, then on all fronts
Mark I Cavalry Carrier	4	29·5	155	Optional armament	6	550 built; France in 1940
Mark I Scout Carrier	4	29·5	155	One 7·7 mm Boys anti-tank rifle, one 7·7 mm Bren gun	3	667 built; France in 1940, then Libya in 1941
Light Tank Mark VI B	5·2	34	130	One ·5-inch m.g., one ·303-inch m.g.	3	France in 1940, then Libya in 1941; later used for artillery observation
Cruisers						
Mark I	12·7	23-25	130	One 2-pounder gun, three ·303-inch m.g.s	6	125 built; used in France, then in North Africa
Mark II	13·7	16	99	As above	4	Limited production. Some service France 1940, western Desert 1941
Mark III	14·5	30	99	One 2-pounder gun, one ·303-inch m.g.	4	Limited production. Some service France 1940, western Desert 1941
Mark IV	14·75	30	93	One 2-pounder gun; one ·303-inch m.g.	4	Limited production until the end of 1941. Some service France 1940, western Desert 1941
Mark VI 'Crusader I'	18	27	99	One 2-pounder gun; one ·303-inch m.g., two 7·92 mm m.g.s	5	North Africa in 1941; 5,300 examples of the three types. Converted into anti-aircraft tanks for the Normandy landings
Mark VI 'Crusader II'	19	27	99	As above	4	
Mark VI 'Crusader III'	19·7	27	99	One 2-pounder or 6-pounder gun; one or two ·303-inch m.g.s	3	
Infantry tanks						
Mark I 'Matilda I'	11	8	69·5	One ·303-inch m.g.	2	Remained in service for first year of Second World War. Afterwards used for training
Mark II 'Matilda II'	26·5	15	69·5	One 2-pounder gun; one 7·92 mm m.g.	4	France in 1940, then North Africa until 1942
Mark III 'Valentine'	16-17	15	90	One 2-pounder (later one 6-pounder) gun; one 7·92 mm m.g.	3-4	8,275 built in all; served in North Africa from 1941 to 1943
Mark IV 'Churchill I-II'	38·5	15·5	87	One 2-pounder gun; or one 3-inch howitzer; plus one 7·92 mm m.g.	5	5,640 built of all versions. First appearance at Dieppe in 1942, then North Africa, Italy, Europe in 1944-5
Mark IV 'Churchill III'	38·5	15·5	87	One 6-pounder gun; one 7·92 mm m.g.	5	
Mark IV 'Churchill V'	38·5	15·5	87	One 95 mm howitzer; one 7·92 mm m.g.	5	

Numerous types of armoured cars were built by the firms of Rolls-Royce, Alvis Crossley, Morris, Humber, Daimler, etc. Hundreds of examples of each mark were produced, and even more in the case of the Daimler models, which totalled 2,694.

1 Operational range without refuelling.

The Royal Air Force

At the end of the First World War Great Britain possessed the most powerful air force in the world: 3,300 front-line aircraft and over 18,000 aircraft of all types, together with an establishment of 290,000 men. With the return of peace it became necessary, of course, to cut down this huge mass of men and machines as quickly as possible, as they would no longer be needed and would prove terribly costly. The new Air Ministry, created in 1918, occupied itself with this task. The force was considerably reduced in size and the number of squadrons cut from one hundred and fifty to twenty-two. The meagre funds now allocated were used principally for the construction of airfields and training and research establishments.

In 1922, however, the number of squadrons was raised to thirty-two, and seven years later to fifty-two. German rearmament hastened this process, and in 1934 Britain began once more to build up an air force worthy of the name, even if it could not reclaim the leading place it had once occupied. In March 1935 its manpower comprised 31,000 regulars and 14,540 reserves, while according to the plans which had been prepared these figures were to be increased to 188,000 and 104,000 respectively by the beginning of 1940.

In 1936 the broad outlines of the future organisation of the RAF were drawn with the creation of the famous 'Commands', those large strategic or administrative formations which bore the following titles:

Fighter Command
Bomber Command
Coastal Command
Transport Command
Balloon Command
Flying Training Command
Technical Training Command
Maintenance Command
Tactical Air Force (Army Cooperation)

All these efforts to bring the RAF up to a level at which it would prove equal to the terrible task awaiting it in 1940 were directed largely by a man who is today almost forgotten: the late Air Marshal Sir Wilfrid Freeman. Without his foresight and imagination, the developments which took place between 1937 and 1939 would never have been achieved and pilots would have been sacrificed in vain.

Each newly created Command was composed of 'Groups' (or aerial divisions), each Group in turn being divided into Wings or squadrons. Each Wing comprised three or four squadrons, which were themselves subdivided into two flights of twelve fighters or eight to ten bombers and designated 'A Flight' and 'B Flight'. From 1940 to 1943 the squadrons or wings were known by the name of their aerodrome, like, for example, the Biggin Hill Wing. Each squadron was numbered, its aircraft being identified with it by means of code-letters painted on the fuselage. Moreover, each aircraft bore its own individual code-letter, allowing the pilot to be identified.

In 1938 the RAF had twenty-five fighter squadrons, sixty-three bomber squadrons, ten army cooperation squadrons, fourteen reconnaissance squadrons and two maritime squadrons, or some 1,750 aircraft in all. By 3 September 1939 the RAF possessed one thousand fighter aircraft, of which a little over half were the new Hurricanes and Spitfires, for between October 1937 and September 1939 the monthly production figures of these two types of fighters, under the impetus provided by Sir Wilfrid Freeman, had increased from twenty-four to forty-four machines in the case of the Hurricane and from thirteen to thirty-two for the Spitfire. Freeman's successor, Lord Beaverbrook, who was appointed Minister of Aircraft Production on 14 May 1940, sped up subsequent development and made possible the following increase in production figures:

TYPE	1940	1941	1942	1943
Heavy bombers	3,679	4,170	4,277	3,113
Light bombers	41	498	1,976	4,614
Fighters	4,283	7,063	9,850	10,727

It was also thanks to Freeman that the RAF was able to make use of a 100 per cent high-quality octane fuel, and that it was eventually equipped with the first really modern bombers, which, three years after the Battle of Britain, were to give Germany a dose of her own medicine.

Each squadron included twenty-five fighter pilots or eighty bomber aircrew in its ranks (although this figure sometimes varied according to the type of aircraft in use) and had a reserve of between ten and twenty men. It can be reckoned that one-third of these aircrew would be NCOs. To the operational aircrew themselves, one must add the scores of fitters, riggers and armourers etc., who had the job of maintaining the aircraft and their weapons.

MACHINE GUNS AND CANNON

A few years earlier machine guns had fired only solid 7·5 mm or 11 mm bullets, but the automatic weapons in service by 1940 had considerably greater power and currently reached calibres of 13·25 mm and 37 mm, normally firing small explosive shells with ultra-sensitive fuses. It goes without saying that the destructive difference between the impact of a solid bullet and that of an explosive shell was enormous. The former, which made a clean hole, was effective only if it hit the pilot or a vital piece of machinery, while the 20 mm cannon shell produced frightful damage to the structure of an aircraft, its splinters alone often cutting control cables or wounding the crew.

Light machine guns, however, still had the advantage over the heavier guns of a more rapid rate of fire, and they raised no serious installation or maintenance problems, their weight and their movement at the moment of firing being relatively limited. At the outbreak of war, heavy automatic weapons were normally located and mounted in the wings of single-engined aircraft, or even—particularly in the case of the 37 mm cannon—in the propeller boss itself. This ingenious method replaced the complicated system of firing through the propeller, which in any case became far too dangerous with the advent of explosive shells. For a long time the bombers retained their turrets with their twin light machine guns, but some aircraft, such as the Halifax, were eventually fitted with a hydraulically operated tail turret armed with four cannon.

During the toughest air fighting of the Battle of Britain, from June to November 1940, the Hurricanes and Spitfires did not have cannon, but instead carried eight ·303-in machine guns in their wings, these being aligned so that their fire would converge. Together they produced a rate of fire of 9,600 rounds a minute. The Messerschmitt Me.109, in comparison, carried two cannon and two 7·9 mm machine guns.

AMMUNITION

The lightest solid bullets weighed just under 1 oz, in 7·5 mm calibre; the heaviest, of 25 mm calibre, could weigh as much as $24\frac{1}{2}$ oz. Metal-based tracer bullets were also provided; whether the gun was belt-or magazine-fed, one round in four would leave a trail of smoke behind it, thus enabling its trajectory to be followed and the aim corrected accordingly.

Explosive bullets and shells were much more elaborate. They contained some 8 to 10 per cent of explosives in proportion to the total weight of the projectile, though there was of course much less in the 'tracers', where the smoke-discharging substance occupied much of the space normally reserved for the charge. The charge was made up of nitrated explosives in powder or strip form, these being stoutly compressed to avoid any 'sinking' due to inertia at the point of discharge. Tetryl, hexogen, pentrite and tolite were currently used; tolite, which was used much less than the others, was normally used in a mixture with them.

ROYAL AIR FORCE I

1. Boulton Paul Defiant — 2. Bristol Beaufighter
Relative speeds of the principal British and German aircraft:
3. Spitfire: 580 km/h — 4. Me.109: 566 km/h — 5. Me.110: 558 km/h — 6. Junkers Ju.88: 548 km/h — 7. Hurricane: 540 km/h — 8. Bristol Beaufighter: 516 km/h — 9. Boulton Paul Defiant: 483 km/h — 10. Dornier Do.215: 467 km/h — 11. Fairey Fulmar: 424 km/h — 12. Dornier Do.17: 408 km/h — 13. Gloster Gladiator: 400 km/h — 14. Heinkel He.111: 395 km/h — 15. Junkers Ju.87 'Stuka': 385 km/h — 16. Blackburn Roc: 315 km/h.

km/h   550   500   450   400   350   300

L. & F. Funcken

Explosive bullets had the advantage of being effective up to distances of half a mile, while the traditional bullet was of very limited use at any range much over two hundred yards. The explosive shell was dangerous to use, particularly aboard bomber aircraft, but it was adjusted so that it would not explode before it had travelled over twenty yards, even if a nervous gunner hit part of his own aircraft while firing at an enemy machine. Another safety precaution ensured that stray projectiles could be automatically destroyed, either by pyrotechnical or mechanical means.

AIRCRAFT

The Hawker Hurricane

The Hawker Hurricane was the RAF's first monoplane fighter. Designed by Sidney Camm of Hawker Aircraft, it first entered squadron service in December 1937. During the great German air offensive in 1940 60 per cent of Fighter Command's squadrons were equipped with Hurricane Mk Is, which at the end of the battle were credited with shooting down nearly half of the 1,733 German aircraft. The Hurricane was, however, somewhat old-fashioned in comparison with its swastika-bedecked opponents, even its 'hump' betraying its descent from the wooden Hawker biplanes. Apart from its handling qualities below twenty thousand feet, it was inferior in every respect to its German counterpart, and was forced to concentrate its attacks on the bomber formations, while covered by the Spitfires.

A top speed of 323 mph is today still attributed to this valiant fighter aircraft, but trials which were carried out under the direction of Air Chief Marshal Sir Hugh Dowding, Commander-in-Chief of Fighter Command, to establish the absolute and relative speeds of his fighters (the Hurricane and Spitfire), revealed an actual maximum speed of about 302 mph for the Hurricane and just over 352 mph for the Spitfire, to which 364 mph was generously conceded. It was this same Dowding who lay behind the introduction of the armoured windscreens fitted to these two fighters. To those who thought that the

likely expense would be too high, Dowding replied: 'If Chicago gangsters can have bullet-proof glass in their cars, I can't see any reason why my pilots should not have the same.'

By the end of September 1940 448 Hurricanes had been lost in combat, and the following month 240 more machines crashed, but by now the enemy had been compelled to give up the struggle. Following this period of the war several new types entered the struggle, including the Hurricane IIB with twelve machine guns and the IIC with its four 20 mm cannon. The Hurricane IID ground-attack variant, with two 40 mm cannon, first saw action in 1942. The Sea Hurricane, a special type for naval air operations, first flew in 1941.[1]

1 Later examples will be discussed in vol. 4.

ROYAL AIR FORCE II

1. Hurricane Mark I — 2. Hurricane IID — 3–4. Standard camouflage schemes — 5. Grey-green camouflage — 6–7. Standard camouflage schemes — 8. Grey-green camouflage — 9. Camouflage for night fighters, 1941 — 10. Roundel used for a limited period in 1939-40 — 11. Fuselage roundel from June 1940 to June 1942 — 12. Roundel used on the upper surface of wings or on the fuselage of bomber aircraft (1923 to 1947)

The Supermarine Spitfire

This fighter made a very strong impression upon the German pilots, quickly gaining a reputation which it was never to lose. It was the most widely produced of all British aircraft, and during a long career lasting a dozen years twenty thousand planes emerged from the factories in forty different variants.

The first Supermarine Spitfire MkI was at least as good as its most determined opponent, the Me.109. It emerged from the drawing-board of Reginald Mitchell, one of the most brilliant aeronautical engineers Britain has ever produced. As early as 1931 Mitchell had created for his employers, the Supermarine Division of Vickers-Armstrong Ltd, a small, thoroughbred seaplane which had triumphed in the famous international competition known as the Schneider Trophy. One aspect of this victory which is not generally known is that it was a generous and eccentric old lady, the very wealthy Lady Houston, and not the Government, who provided the necessary £50,000. The trophy was won with a speed of 403 mph, and it was decided to exploit the military potential of this thoroughbred. Six months after the appearance of the Me.109 in Germany, the first Spitfire prototype was unveiled in March 1936.

The introduction of the Rolls-Royce Merlin engine and the change from the variable-pitch to the constant-speed airscrew—a development wrung from officialdom by the aviation pioneer Geoffrey de Havilland—made the Spitfire a very worthy adversary to the famous Luftwaffe fighter. Another significant improvement was the adoption of a new carburettor, which replaced the old floating type. The latter could not stand up to the rapid manoeuvres necessary in aerial combat, and German pilots had previously been able to escape by sudden nose-dives in which the British pilots had been unable to follow them.

Eighteen Spitfire squadrons were ready for operations in June 1940; this figure had risen to nineteen by the following month. The critical months of August and September saw these squadrons suffer serious blows, 248 of their machines being destroyed and a further 135 damaged. But they had borne the full weight of the aggressive German fighter arm almost single-handed.

The Boulton Paul Defiant

When it appeared in August 1937, this two-seat fighter embodied a tactical conception which was quite different from the classic technique of air fighting. This lay in the curious arrangement of its armament, which comprised four ·303-in machine guns grouped together in a single turret. The basic idea of its designers was that the pilot would now only have to concern himself with flying the aircraft while the gunner would be free to blast away at the enemy with guns which were capable of traversing through 360°. Moreover, the Defiant could, in theory, attack enemy bombers from the beam and thus avoid having to face the powerful frontal armament with which the latter were generally equipped. In fact the whole idea proved disastrous. Far from being relieved, the pilot found himself continually concerned with the task of placing his gunner in the best possible position in relation to the target. Having to decide every course of action with this in mind, he was almost entirely subservient to the demands of his fellow crew-member.

The Defiant's first encounter with the enemy, a Ju.88, resulted in victory; but the next day the destruction of four Ju.87s was followed by the slaughter of five out of six Defiants at the hands of the German fighter escort. The Defiants registered a few more victories—fourteen in fact—a little later, but subsequent encounters proved so costly that they were withdrawn from the battle, to be used more successfully as night fighters until the beginning of 1942, and ending their career as target-towing aircraft for gunnery training.

The Bristol Blenheim

Beginning the series of heavier aircraft, the Bristol Blenheim was introduced in 1937 as a medium bomber, but it equipped six Fighter Command

ROYAL AIR FORCE III

1. Spitfire Mark I, 1939 — 2. Spitfire Mark VB, 1942 — 3–4. Standard camouflage schemes — 5–7. Silhouettes of the Hurricane, Spitfire and Me.109
Evolution of camouflage and markings: 8. May 1939 — 9. October 1939 — 10. September 1940 — 11. January 1941 — 12. August 1942

squadrons following the adoption of four ·303-in machine guns in a ventral pàck beneath the fuselage. As daylight operations became virtually suicidal, the fighter version of the Blenheim was turned into a night fighter, in which role it constituted the backbone of the newly formed night interception force of the RAF.

The Bombers

Among the bombers, the following twin-engined types must be mentioned:

Vickers Wellington: One of the most remarkable aircraft of the whole war, with fantastic powers of endurance. It entered service in 1938 and carried out the first raid of the war in 1939. Eleven thousand five hundred Wellingtons of all types were built.

Handley Page Hampden: Delivered to the RAF in 1938, this aircraft, which was classed as a heavy bomber at the time of its introduction, lacked adequate defensive armament and ceased to be used operationally in 1942. Fifteen hundred were built.

Bristol Beaufort: From 1939 onwards this aircraft saw service in every major campaign and in every theatre of operations as a torpedo aircraft. Twelve hundred were built.

Among the four-engined types, the following must be mentioned:

Armstrong Whitworth Whitley: This was the aircraft which carried out the first raid on Berlin in 1939, and it was to serve as a night bomber until 1942. Fifteen hundred examples of its main production version, the Mk V, were built.

Handley Page Halifax: In 1939 this became the second heavy bomber to enter service with the RAF. It served with distinction in Europe and, alone of its kind, in the Middle East.

Avro Lancaster: This aircraft entered service in 1942. One of the most famous bombers to attack Germany, Lancasters sank the *Tirpitz* and breached the Ruhr dams. Seven thousand four hundred were built.

In Coastal Command, that great force which performed innumerable services but which is too often forgotten, the following famous aircraft were to be found:

Consolidated Catalina: This aircraft first appeared in the United States in 1935, and was to serve as a long-range convoy escort, in an anti-submarine role or as transport and rescue aircraft. Over six hundred and fifty were built for the RAF.

Short Sunderland: First built in England in 1937, this aircraft was the first to sink a German submarine in 1940. It served both in the evacuation of threatened bases in Norway and Crete, and as a transport aircraft. Powerfully armed, in some versions with twelve machine guns and two cannon—this particular version nicknamed the 'Flying Porcupine'—it shot down a good many enemy bombers. Production continued until 1945, seven hundred and twenty-one being produced in all.

ROYAL AIR FORCE IV

1. Bristol Blenheim — 2. Vickers Wellington — 3. Short Stirling — 4. Avro Lancaster — 5. Pilot's brevet or 'Wings', worn on the left breast — 6. Observer's brevet — 7. Air Gunner's brevet — 8. Service dress cap of a Marshal of the Royal Air Force, with badge enlarged to show detail — 9. Service dress cap of a Group Captain, with badge enlarged. The same badge was also worn on the caps of lower-ranking officers (figure 10) — 11. Service dress cap, with badge enlarged, as worn by NCOs — 12. Officer's field service cap (forage or duty cap), with insignia enlarged — 13. Sleeve rank insignia of a Marshal of the Royal Air Force — 14. Air Chief Marshal — 15. Air Marshal — 16. Air Vice-Marshal — 17. Air Commodore — 18. Group Captain — 19. Wing Commander — 20. Squadron Leader — 21. Flight Lieutenant — 22. Flying Officer — 23. Pilot Officer

ROYAL AIR FORCE V (page 36)

1. Bristol Beaufort — 2. Handley Page Hampden — 3. Armstrong-Whitworth Whitley — 4. Handley Page Halifax — 5. Westland Lysander — 6. Officer — 7. Airman (other ranks) — 8. NCO (Flight Sergeant)
Arm insignia: 9. Warrant Officer — 10. Flight Sergeant — 11. Sergeant — 12. Corporal — 13. Leading Aircraftman — 14. Wireless Operator — 15. Air Gunner — 16. Physical Training Instructor — 17. Apprentice and Boy Entrant — 18. Drum Major — 19. Field service cap (forage or duty cap) for NCOs and airmen (other ranks), with badge enlarged

ROYAL AIR FORCE VI (page 37)

1. Catalina — 2. Sunderland — 3. Anson — 4. Walrus — 5. Air Gunner from a bomber crew — 6. American volunteer pilot wearing the uniform of the Royal Naval Volunteer Reserve

13

14

15

16

17

18

1

2

3

4

5

6

7

8

9

10

11

12

19

20

21

22

23

L. & F. Funcken

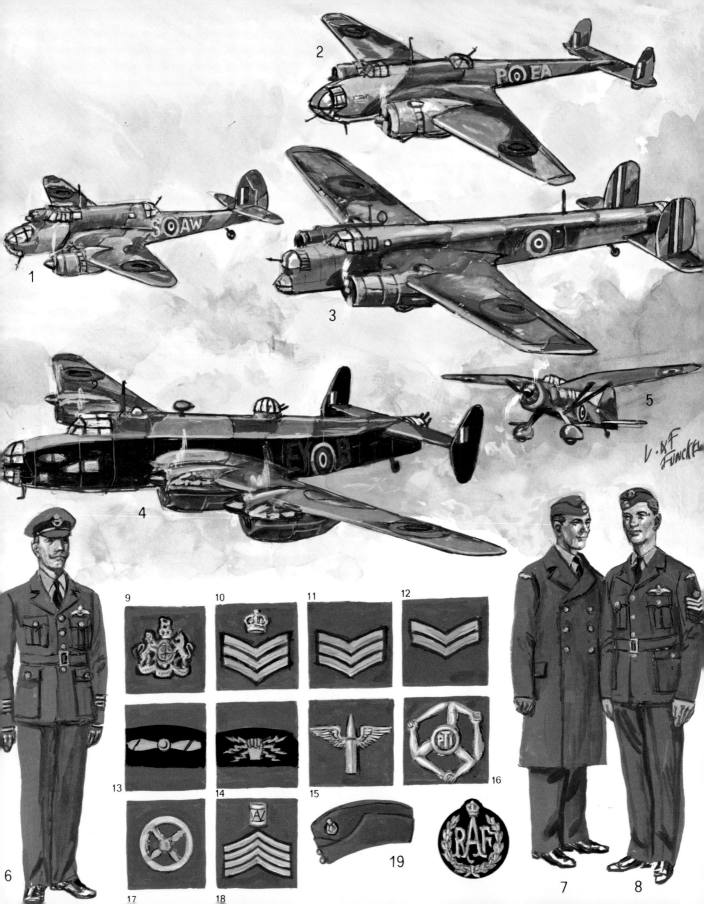

1

2

3

4

5

6

7

8

9

10

11

12

13

14

15

16

17

18

19

1

2

3

4

5

6

ARMOURED VEHICLES AND AIRCRAFT

Russian Armoured Vehicles

At the end of the First World War the Soviet government had entrusted some of its best engineers with the task of developing powerful assault tanks and putting them into service. The only tanks in Russia in the early 1920s were the British Mark Vs and the French Renault FT17s captured from the White army, and it was 1924 before factories capable of making such a thing as a reasonably sophisticated tank became operational. The first Russian assault tank was completed in 1927 and was christened MS1—*Maliy Soprovozdieniya*—or more popularly T18. It was in fact an up-dated version of the little Renault FT. This tank was immediately followed by a medium-weight tank of the same type, but neither tank registered much real progress on First World War tanks and production of them was stopped in 1928.

In 1930-32 Great Britain and the United States both produced several tanks which were well received in the Soviet Union. The Vickers six-ton tank and the small but excellent Vickers-Carden-Loyd vehicle were copied on a large scale and provided the light T26A, B and C tanks, as well as the two-seater Bren gun carrier minus turret, known as the T27. Although of little fighting value this latter vehicle was to prove very useful in the development of a tank service corps, as well as providing an excellent test piece for an emergent Soviet industry faced for the first time with the difficulties of large-scale production lines. The American tank, invented by that engineer extraordinary J. Walter Christie, also gave rise to a series of tanks from the Russian production lines which were equally well received. The series took the name *Bystrochodya Tank*—fast tank—abbreviated to

BT2, 5 and 7. These T26s and BTs were produced in large numbers and a great many were used to equip the Soviet forces from 1932 until the end of 1941.

Two heavy tanks were subsequently studied and produced, this time without the benefit of foreign models. Both carried multiple turrets capable of firing from every angle in order to ensure that the infantry had the support of their powerful fire at all times. With these 'group manoeuvres tanks' the Russians demonstrated their confidence in the theories then being propounded in France—theories which were to be completely overturned in May 1940. These monsters, which weighed between twenty-eight and thirty tons, were produced under the names T28 medium and T35 heavy.

In 1940 two new types of armoured vehicle quietly made their appearance, the T34 medium and the heavy KV—*Klementy Voroshilov*—two notable examples of a completely new generation of tanks. Unfortunately the Russians had only got as far as issuing their forces with one hundred and fifteen of the T34s and two hundred and thirty of the KVs before the Germans launched their attack on 22 June 1941.

STRATEGY

The number of AFVs possessed by the Soviet army when the Germans attacked has been estimated at twenty thousand. However, ten thousand must immediately be deducted from this impressive figure, as representing their reserve forces, and of the ten

SOVIET ARMOURED VEHICLES, 1939-1941 I

1. T26 A — 2. T27 — 3. T28 — 4. Tank crew's helmet — 5. Lieutenant, armoured vehicles — 6. Collar patches worn on the leather jacket and on the loose shirt underneath it

1

2

3

4

5

6

L. & F. Funcken

SUMMARY TABLE OF THE MAIN SOVIET ARMOURED VEHICLES FROM 1927-41

TYPE	TONNAGE	SPEED	RANGE	ARMS	CREW	WHERE USED
MS1-T18	5.5	17 km/h	60 km	1 37 mm cannon, 1 7.6 mm machine gun	2	
T26A	8.6	30 km/h	140 km	2 7.62 mm machine guns	3	Manchuria, Finland, then Russia until 1942
T26B	9.4	28 km/h	375 km	1 45 mm cannon, 1 or 2 7.62 mm machine guns	3	
T26C	10.3	27 km/h	225 km	1 45 mm cannon, 2/3 7.62 mm machine guns	3	
T27 T27A T27B	2.7	40 km/h as above but slightly more spacious as above with improvements to ventilation and vision	120 km	1 7.62 mm machine gun	2	Types A & B during the war in Finland; then as artillery tractors or self-propelling cannons in 1941.
BT2	10.2	approx. 70 km/h on wheels, 55 km/h on tracks		1 37 mm cannon, 1 7.62 mm machine gun	3	Rarely used on wheels—all three used in Spain, Manchuria and Finland, then against German invasion in 1941
BT5	11.5			1 45 mm cannon, 1 7.62 mm machine gun	3	
BT7	13.8			1 45 mm cannon, 1-3 machine guns	3	
T28	28	37 km/h	220 km	1 76.2 mm howitzer, 1-4 7.62 mm machine guns	6	Finland, then Russia in 1941
T35	35	30 km/h	150 km	1 76.2 mm cannon, 2 45 mm cannons, 5 7.62 mm machine guns	10	At most 30 were made; Finland, and Russia in 1941
SMK and T100	56-58	not known		1 76.2 mm cannon, 1 45 mm cannon, 3 7.62 mm machine guns	6/7	Tested in Finland then abandoned
KV1 A	43.5	35 km/h	355 km	1 76.2 mm cannon, 3 7.62 mm machine guns	5	Finland then Russia in 1941
KV1 B	47.5	35 km/h	335 km	1 76.2 mm cannon, 3 7.62 mm machine guns	5	
KV2 A	52	26 km/h	250 km	1 152 mm howitzer, 3 7.62 mm machine guns	6	
T34	26.3	53 km/h	400 km	1 76.2 mm cannon, 2 7.62 mm machine guns	4	Russia in July 1941

thousand in active service the greater number were already of out-moded design, badly armoured, badly armed, and with engines that had seen better days. Finally, not more than 40 per cent of these remaining vehicles were in any real fighting condition, and there were a mere 1,450 vehicles of the latest type. It is not difficult, then, to understand how some three thousand seven hundred German AFVs, which were rolling into Russian territory from June to October 1941, were able to destroy or capture between fifteen and eighteen thousand Russian vehicles.

The doubtful quality of many of the Russian vehicles, however, does not entirely explain this incredible carnage, as on the German side too the armoured vehicles were far from being thoroughly up-to-date; still in use, for example, were the small 38T Czechs and the Panzers I and II. The real reason for the success of the Wehrmacht lay in the superiority of their armoured vehicle strategy rather than in any greater strength of weapons. In Russia theory on the use of tanks had been totally re-thought after the misinterpreted events of the Spanish Civil War; the idea of the armoured corps had been pushed into the background and the old concept of the tank working in conjunction with the infantrymen taken up again.

SOVIET ARMOURED VEHICLES, 1939-1941 II

1. BT 5 — 2. BT 7 — 3. T35 — 4. SMK

1

2

3

4

L. x F. Funcken

The disastrous experiences of the war in Finland, and German successes in Poland and France, had finally brought about a swing back to mechanised units, and in November 1940 twenty-two mechanised corps, each with two tank divisions and one motorised division, were created; but it would have needed far more than the seven months which remained before the German invasion for these precious divisions to be organised and equipped. The majority had to fight with only two-thirds of the regulation equipment, and some of the teams in the most modern tanks had had no more than a few hours training before they found themselves in combat.

Caught in the middle of this full-scale reorganisation, the Soviet army could only withdraw in the face of the German onslaught. Struggling in small groups, the old-fashioned Russian tanks were literally wiped out by the powerful fire from the German armoured columns, to such an extent that General Halder, chief of German HQ, estimated that the campaign in Russia would be over in a fortnight. At the price of unprecedented sacrifice and suffering, however, the Russians, whom the whole world thought had been totally beaten, managed to halt the German onrush, the new T34, BT1 and BT2 tanks, much less vulnerable to the German tank fire, being the main cause of this initial check to the enemy. The terrible Russian winter, an invaluable additional ally, now set in. The front settled down, leaving immense stretches of territory in the hands of the enemy. But their conquests had cost them very dearly. In the first twenty-seven days of the invasion alone they had lost at least half of their three thousand seven hundred tanks.

SOVIET ARMOURED VEHICLES, 1939-1941 III

1. KV1 A — 2. Bronniford BA armoured car — 3. KV 2 — 4. Field cap — 5. Cap, NCOs and officers — 6. Soldier in summer dress

1

2

3

4

5

6

L. ✗ F. Funcken

Belgian Armoured Vehicles

Belgium did not, as many military writers have falsely stated, shrink from the heavy expense involved in purchasing AFVs. The Belgian cavalry began to motorise its units in 1936, a conversion which was to cost over two hundred million Belgian francs. Four types of armoured vehicle were developed, based on the Vickers-Carden-Loyd chassis used in the British and French 1935 model Renault ACG, though the first two types showed considerable differences in bodywork and armament. The first and lighter model weighed thirteen tons and was known as the T13. It had one Belgian anti-tank gun (47 mm) strongly protected at the front by an enveloping shield, which, however, left the rear completely open. It was really a self-propelling cannon. The second type, the fifteen-ton T15, had a heavy machine gun, the ·5-inch Vickers, under a turret which gave all-round protection. A third type, a small machine-gun carrier, was used for the transportation of munitions and for pulling the 47 mm anti-tank gun. The fourth type weighed sixteen tons and used the French Renault chassis. Although this was a real tank it was called the *auto blindée du corps de cavalerie* (cavalry corps armoured car) or more commonly ABCC. It had a revolving gun turret with a 47 mm gun and a ·5-inch machine gun.

The Belgian AFV forces totalled about two hundred machines, of which twenty-three were the heavy sixteen-ton tanks. For some strange reason these sixteen-tonners were disliked by the experts, having been tried out in 1937, found wanting, and pushed into a corner of the factory until 1939, to be rediscovered after the startling performance of the *Panzerdivisionen* in Poland. Only eight of them were in even a remotely serviceable state, and these were promptly divided between the 1st regiment of Guides and the 2nd Lancers regiment. Against all reason these tanks were put into service, in spite of the fact that they were generally badly equipped and were even without radio. Inevitably they were wiped out, one after the other, in a completely unequal fight, although the twenty-four soldiers who manned them fought a tremendous battle which is now little remembered.

The smaller T13s and T15s met the same fate, the last of them appearing on the Lys, badly damaged, but battling on against the lines of machine guns right up to the eighteenth day of that desperate struggle.

BELGIAN ARMOURED VEHICLES, 1939-1940

1. T13 with anti-tank gun (47 mm) — 2. 2T15, 3rd Lancers regiment, with Vickers machine gun (·5-inch) — 3. Cavalry corps armoured car with cannon (47 mm) and machine gun (·5-inch) — 4. Tank crew — 5. Detail of helmet

The French Air Force

In 1930 the French military authorities were to announce in tones of supreme confidence: 'The time has come to state in all honesty that the French air force is the best in the world.' Best, that is, in the sense that it was unrivalled by the British air force, which it was using as its standard of reference. Yet only five years later the French air force had to draw on vast credit to replace its equipment, since even its newest machines could not now compare in performance even with commercial planes. The fighters Dewoitine D.500 and D.501 were now adopted, a decision which moved experts to predict long periods of unemployment in the French aeronautical industry, as the planes were thought to be good for at least ten years. But hardly had they been put into service before they too became outdated and it became necessary to buy the now indispensable modern fighters from the United States. Those chosen were the Curtiss Hawk 75s.

Later in the 1930s tests were completed on a new machine, the Morane-Saulnier MS.406, which was to become numerically the most important aircraft (1,070 went into service) in the French squadrons. Subsequently a Dewoitine D.520 emerged from the factories of the *Société nationale de constructions aéronautiques du Midi* (National Company for Aeronautical Construction in the South). This aeroplane was warmly received, but it was so slow in production that its use in battle was limited to 210 units. Numerous other prototypes were under study in several important firms, such as *Bloch Constructions aéronautiques de l'Ouest, Caudron-Renault, Constructions aéronautiques du Nord, Constructions aéronautiques du Sud-Est,* etc. None of these prototypes, however, apart from the Caudron C.714, managed to get beyond testing stage before war broke out. With the first confrontations it became clear that the Germans had the superiority in speed, compensated for on the French side by better manoeuvrability. The Curtiss was found to be the least satisfactory because of its slow acceleration caused by its large air-cooled engine.

UNIFORMS

The air force was divided into aircrew and ground crew. Cadet officers were trained mainly in the flying schools at Salon-de-Provence, Versailles-Villacoublay, Istres and Rochefort. The officers had four uniforms, which are described in the table overleaf. Flying dress consisted of a long jacket and trousers in brown leather with a leather helmet. When flying the airman had to tuck his jacket inside the belt of his trousers in order to be able to adjust his parachute harness.

FRENCH AIR FORCE, 1939-1940 I

1. Morane — 2. Dewoitine — 3. Brevet, pilot — 4. Brevet for aircrews or crews of airships, mechanics, machine gunners, bombers, photographers, etc. — 5. Mechanics' arm insignia — 6. Record of direct hits scored during the 'phoney war' — 7. Général de brigade in full dress — 8. Corporal pennon-bearer for an air base — 9. NCO, colonial air force — 10. Pilot NCO in town dress. Collar patches of non-commissioned flying officers — 11. Pilot or reconnaissance observer — 12. Machine gunner, and radio operator — 13. Bomber mechanic — 14. Collar patches of NCOs: colonial air force — 15. North African troops — 16. North African ground personnel — 17. Mixed flight — 18. Air bases — 19. Meteorological companies

	TYPE OF GARMENT	RANK MARKS, BUTTONS, INSIGNIA, SHOULDER ORNAMENT	FACINGS	WAISTCOAT	TROUSERS	OVERCOAT	CAP	DAGGER
Officers Evening dress	dark-blue mess dress	blue shoulder straps with gold embroidery; gold insignia, rank marks and no.	rounded, gold embroidery	white	dark blue, blue embroidered stripe	dark-blue cape	dark blue, gold embroidery	—
Full dress	dark-blue frock coat	heavy gold cord on shoulders; gold buttons, insignia and rank marks	special embroidery for general officers	dark blue	dark blue	dark-blue overcoat	dark blue, gold embroidery	white sheath
Walking-out dress	dark-blue frock coat	as for full dress but no heavy cord	stripes	—	dark blue	dark blue	as for full dress without stripe	as above
Working dress and field service dress	dark-blue frock coat	as for walking-out dress	as for walking-out dress	—	breeches and boots	dark blue	as for walking-out dress	as above
Adjudants-chefs and adjudants (no evening dress)	dark-blue frock coat	as above without cord	stripes	—	dark-blue trousers	dark blue	—	as above
Sous-officiers Full dress	dark-blue frock coat	as above without cord	gold chevrons	—	dark blue	dark blue	false chin strap in gold	—
Corporals and lance-corporals Full dress	dark-blue frock coat	—	orange wool chevrons	—	dark blue	dark blue	—	—
Sous-officiers and ranks Walking-out dress	grey-blue pea-jacket; orange number and collar ornament (gold for NCOs)	gold buttons	—	—	grey-blue	grey-blue	grey-blue	—
Working dress and field service dress	short leather coat; collar as above	bronze buttons	—	—	grey-blue	grey-blue	dark-blue beret and helmet	—

FRENCH AIR FORCE, 1939-1940 II

1. Curtiss 75A — 2. Caudron C.714 — 3. Drummer, air force regiment — 4. Mechanic — 5. Airman in summer flying suit made of linen. Prototypes: 6. Potez 230 — 7. Bloch MB.155 — 8. CAO.200 — 9. SE.100

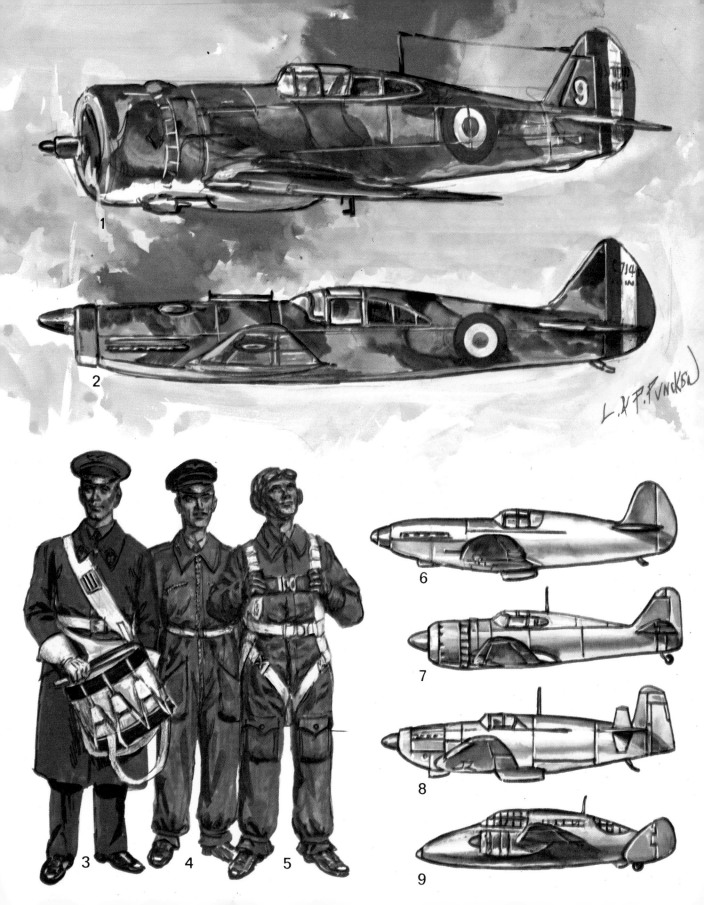

1

2

L.&P.Runcke

3 4 5

6

7

8

9

THE FRENCH AIR FORCE IN BATTLE

No force has ever been so viciously slandered as was the French air force during and after the Second World War, the slander stemming from the first days of the disastrous 1940 campaign. One of the most deeply rooted beliefs is that throughout this period it was completely absent from the skies, which were thus left open to the German squadrons. The truth is quite different; the numbers of airmen wounded or killed in this period speak for themselves. The French air force recorded 776 dead, 180 missing and 537 wounded, some 30 per cent of the total flying force. In passing, it is worth remarking in this context that unlike armies and navies the number of air force men killed in battle is usually greater than the number of wounded.

Estimates of the total number of planes possessed by the French at the outbreak of the war vary greatly, ranging from 1,200 to 3,861 modern machines. For fighters alone the figures are equally variable, again ranging from 360, 418, 570, 580 to 900 planes, a confusion which makes it impossible to define exactly how many fighters joined in the engagements, how many were in immediate reserve, and how many were situated on more distant airfields. It would seem best to refer to some recently published figures which give the following approximate numbers:

600 Bloch 151 and 152, Morane 406, Curtiss H.75, and Dewoitine 530 *single-seater fighters*
100 Potez 630 and 63/I *multi-seater fighters*
175 Bréguet 693, Lioré and Olivier 451, Amiot 354, and Martin 167 *bombers*
400 Potez 637 and 63/II, and Bloch 174 *reconnaissance planes*
8 Farman 224 *troop transport planes*

giving a total of 1,283 machines ready for immediate use.

From 10 to 15 May 1940 two hundred and fifty single-seaters and forty two-seaters, together with one hundred bombers and another hundred reconnaissance planes, engaged the Germans in combat. Fighting mainly in the skies over Belgium, they opposed one thousand Messerschmitt 109s, two hundred and fifty Me.110s, and one thousand five hundred and eighty bombers, of which three hundred and eighty were Ju.87 'Stukas', backed up by about five hundred German intelligence planes. The French fighters, usually sent up in small groups of six to nine planes, had to take on enemy formations of at least sixteen units, all of superior quality at least technically.

Defective radio communications made the effective intervention of the French air force slow and sometimes impossible. Cooperation with ground forces, again made extremely difficult by this same lack of radio communications, was further hampered by the absence of any seriously thought-out tactics. Indeed some squadron leaders cleared a path by hedge-hopping, simply to prove to the infantry that the air force was really there—senseless behaviour which cost the lives of several pilots, who were shot down by the very people whose morale they were supposed to be raising. The French fighters, then, were not only numerically inferior and technically less well supported, but they also lacked the speed of their German counterparts, the Me.109, for example, being able to achieve 80 km per hour more than the Morane 406. The French also carried inferior fire power, with only one 20 mm gun and two machine guns as against the two 20 mm guns and three machine guns of the German plane. It is also true, however, that these differences were considerably less marked with the Bloch and the Dewoitine. As regards crew, the French had a good deal of flying experience but were not experienced in warfare, whereas since the Spanish Civil War the Germans had a good many pilots who possessed this experience.

In spite of many individual acts of bravery these deficiencies, combined with a serious lack of manpower, could not be overcome, and after five days of intensive battle in the Belgian skies the French air force was forced to withdraw to France where the German AFVs had by now broken through. The sacrifices made by the French and Belgian airmen were quickly forgotten, with the slander of the French air force over its performance in 1940 as a consequence, but the facts speak for themselves. A great deal of

FRENCH AIR FORCE, 1939-1940 III

1. Potez 63/I — 2. Potez 63/II — 3. Lioré and Olivier — 4. CAO.700, prototype

1

2

3

4

L. & F. Funcken

accurate detail has been produced by Belgian researchers to prove how deeply involved the French air force was in the fighting. Of the sixty-four aircraft twenty-nine Moranes were brought down over Belgian territory, and a further thirty-two were lost beyond the Belgian frontier, or in unspecified parts of the country. Those five days of war cost the lives of forty-two French airmen, and a further twenty-two who managed to escape death were captured by the Germans.[1]

The deaths of these French and Allied airmen, however, were not completely in vain, for at least one hundred and seventy-three wrecked German aircraft were found on Belgian ground; it is reasonable to assess the German losses at about two hundred machines, including those shot down by the DCA.

In the French skies the battles followed the same course. The hopelessly outdated method of liaison which connected General Gamelin's HQ at Vincennes to the Commander of Operations at La Ferte-sous Jouarre east of Paris and to GHQ at Montry,[2] not only had no radio but, even more shatteringly, not even a teleprinter. In the circumstances it is hardly surprising that it took at least six hours to alert the air force and to give them details of specific missions; and that an order emanating from the general in chief had to be allowed forty-eight hours for transmission. Throughout this period the air force carried out its duties as best it could, but the Battle of France came to a close with the French having lost one-third of their flying manpower. The last machine to fall from the French skies was a Morane-Saulnier piloted by Lieutenant Raphenne, bringing the number of fighters lost to three hundred and six; on the other hand the wreckages of twelve hundred enemy aircraft[3] bore witness to the ferocity of the combat which had taken place.

These heavy German losses were to allow the British a breathing space before their test of strength came, and seriously to deprive Germany of a precious part of her aerial forces in the Battle of Britain.

1 These details have been taken from the Belgian military aviation review *Wings*, in an article entitled 'The French air force in Belgium in May 1940'.
2 South of Meaux.
3 Of which about two hundred were brought down by the DCA and exactly nine hundred and nineteen by French fighters.

The German Air Force 1939-1941

THE MESSERSCHMITT 109

The Luftwaffe was reborn in 1934 with astonishing enthusiasm, the result of intensive work carried out over a long period by various highly skilled engineers. Among these was Professor W. Messerschmitt, who had created a single-seater fighter, which was destined to be manufactured in larger numbers than any other machine of its type, and eventually to constitute more than three-fifths of the total number of German fighting planes. The first prototype made its maiden flight in 1935. The Me.109 went through several models before attracting world notice, but by 1939 it had come to be regarded as the best fighter plane in Europe.

This evolution of the Messerschmitt is sufficiently important to merit further discussion. In January 1936, five months after the Messerschmitt's maiden flight, a second model was tested, and then a third in June of the same year. The problem of arms was difficult to solve and several schemes were tried out

GERMAN AIR FORCE, 1939-1941 I

Collar patches and shoulder straps: 1. Reichsmarschall — 2. Generalfeldmarschall — 3. Generaloberst — 4. General der Flieger — 5. Generalleutnant — 6. Generalmajor — 7. Oberst — 8. Oberstleutnant — 9. Major — 10. Hauptmann — 11. Oberleutnant — 12. Leutnant — 13. Stabsfeldwebel — 14. Oberfeldwebel — 15. Feldwebel — 16. Unterfeldwebel — 17. Unteroffizier — 18. Hauptgefreiter — 19. Obergefreiter — 20. Gefreiter — 21. Soldier
NB: The colours of the different services are described in the text.
22. Flying helmet — 23. Special national emblem worn on the breast — 24. Shield in national colours worn on the right side of the helmet — 25. Parachute troops' helmet — 26. National emblem worn on the left side of the helmet — 27. Officer's cap — 28. Pilot's brevet — 29. *ibid.* for observers — 30. *ibid.* for army parachute troops (disbanded in 1939) — 31. *ibid.* for Luftwaffe parachute troops — 32. Luftwaffe paratrooper in walking-out dress — 33. Officer of the Condor Legion (Spanish Civil War) — 34. Flak NCO — 35. Major in full dress — 36. Paratrooper in jumping dress

before the first 109B in the series was issued to a fighter squadron in 1937. The machine continued to evolve under the codes BF[1].109B2, CO, C1 and C2. Then in 1938 the last two models were sent to Spain, where the Condor legion was fighting on General Franco's side, to replace the first B2s which had been sent there in 1937. Although it continued to be modified, the Messerschmitt became the standard fighter in the Luftwaffe, under the name Me.109E, in the autumn of 1939. It was this machine which fought in Poland, then in the west in 1940, and finally in the famous Battle of Britain.

Superior in most respects to all enemy fighters, the Me.109s gave the Allied pilots a difficult time. Nevertheless, they were unable to bring victory to the German forces in the English skies, not only because of the heroism of the British defence but also because of their short range, which prevented them from prolonged raiding. Many of the pilots came down in the Channel through not keeping a close watch on their fuel gauges.

Throughout this period the engineers had continued their researches, and eventually they perfected a new model, of very sophisticated technology, the Me.109F, which was ready to go into service in January 1941. Yet more variants were subsequently created (the subject of a later chapter in this volume).

THE MESSERSCHMITT 110

Designed to fly with bombers and cover their action, as well as to take on the role of strategic fighter, the Me.110 *Zerstörer* (destroyer) appeared in 1939 in the *Zerstörergruppen* of the Luftwaffe. This machine had gone through several versions before being considered operational, and variants existed which were used either as fighter bombers or as reconnaissance fighters—when they were not being used as glider towing planes! By 1940 the Luftwaffe had more than a thousand of these Me.110s, but they were definitely a less successful plane than their little brothers the Me.109s, particularly over Britain, where these escort planes had themselves to be escorted by Me.109s, such was their inferiority compared with the British

fighters. Nor did the arrival of the new Me.110C put right this deficiency. Numerous different types continued to be produced right up until the end of 1944,[2] when the last models came out of the factories.

THE JUNKERS JU.87 'Stuka'

With this very specialised aircraft the Germans introduced a completely new dimension to bombers. The full name of this bomber was the *Sturzkampfflugzeug*, or more conveniently the 'Stuka', and it was to become notorious during the campaigns in Poland and France because of its spectacular dives and the sinister wail of its siren. It was designed in 1933 by the engineer Hermann Pohlmann, and was incorporated into the air force in 1937 under the registration Ju.87A. There were the inevitable modifications, and the Stuka which took part in Hitler's war operations was the Ju.87B model.

After the success of the dive-bombing attacks in 1939 and 1940, the *Stukagruppen* attempted the same tactics over British territory; this time, however, they were met with an aggressive and well organised fighter force and sustained severe losses. The Stuka was

2 See page 114 in this volume and vol. 4.

GERMAN AIR FORCE, 1939-1941 II

1–2. Me. 109 — 3. Me. 109 B-2, Condor Legion (Spanish Civil War) — 4. Me. 109 E4B — 5–7. Various kinds of camouflage — 8–12. Squadron insignia

1 *Bayerische Flugzeugwerke.*

withdrawn from battle, though it was later to be successful again in the Balkans and in Russia, at least during the early months. Its task, however, became increasingly difficult to carry out and production of the Stuka finally ceased in 1944.[1]

THE JUNKERS JU.88 BOMBER

This twin-engined AI type bomber went into service at the beginning of hostilities. The first squadrons thus equipped played a relatively minor role on the western front, but in the Battle of Britain it established itself as the best bomber in the Luftwaffe.

THE DORNIER DO.17 AND DO.215 BOMBERS

The Do.17, whose slim silhouette won it the name of the 'flying pencil', was well known for its victory in the 1937 international competition, 'The Circuit of the Alps'. The Do.17Z was the first of a long series produced from 1938 onwards, the version destined for foreign markets being the Do.215, which appeared in 1939.

The Do.215 and Do.17Z models, with their dive bomb attacks on naval traffic and their low altitude surprise attacks, performed brilliantly in the Battle of Britain, but the widespread use of the Do.17 ceased when the decision was made to call off the operation which was to have brought Britain to her knees.

THE HEINKEL HE.111

Elegant and powerful, the twin-engined He.111 proved itself a particularly well designed bomber in its time, but it was already a little out of date even at the beginning of the war. The He.111 went into service in 1936 and was to undergo a whole series of modifications, the types H and O emerging as the models which made up the greater part of the *Kampfgruppen* of 1939. Of all the German bombers, the He.111 was the one which suffered the most over enemy territory.

1 Later versions of the Stuka will be described on page 118.

Table of Comparative Maximum Speeds of French and German Planes.

FIGHTERS		km per hour
Germany :	Messerschmitt 109	566
	Messerschmitt 110	558
France :	Dewoitine D.520	535
	Curtiss H.75	500
	Morane-Saulnier 406	485
	Potez 63/I	440
	Nieuport 622	250
BOMBERS		
Germany :	Heinkel 111	395
	Junkers 87 'Stuka'	385
	Junkers 88	548
	Dornier 17	408
	Dornier 215	467
France :	Lioré and Olivier	465
	Potez 63/II	425

It is impossible to fix accurate figures for the German forces in 1940 but the following is a reasonable estimate:

fighters	1,000
bombers	1,800
reconnaissance	400

GERMAN AIR FORCE, 1939-1941 III

1. Me.110 — 2. Ju.87 — 3. Ju.88 A — 4. Comparative sizes of these three aircraft — 5. Breast insignia of pilot observer Marks of rank on flying clothes, overalls or waterproofs: 6. Generalfeldmarschall and Generaloberst — 7. General der Flieger — 8. Generalleutnant — 9. Generalmajor — 10. Oberst — 11. Oberstleutnant — 12. Major — 13. Hauptmann — 14. Oberleutnant — 15. Leutnant — 16. Stabsfeldwebel — 17. Oberfeldwebel — 18. Feldwebel — 19. Unterfeldwebel — 20. Unteroffizier — 21. Flieger-Hauptingenieur — 22. Flieger-Oberingenieur — 23. Flieger-Ingenieur — 24. Airman in flying dress

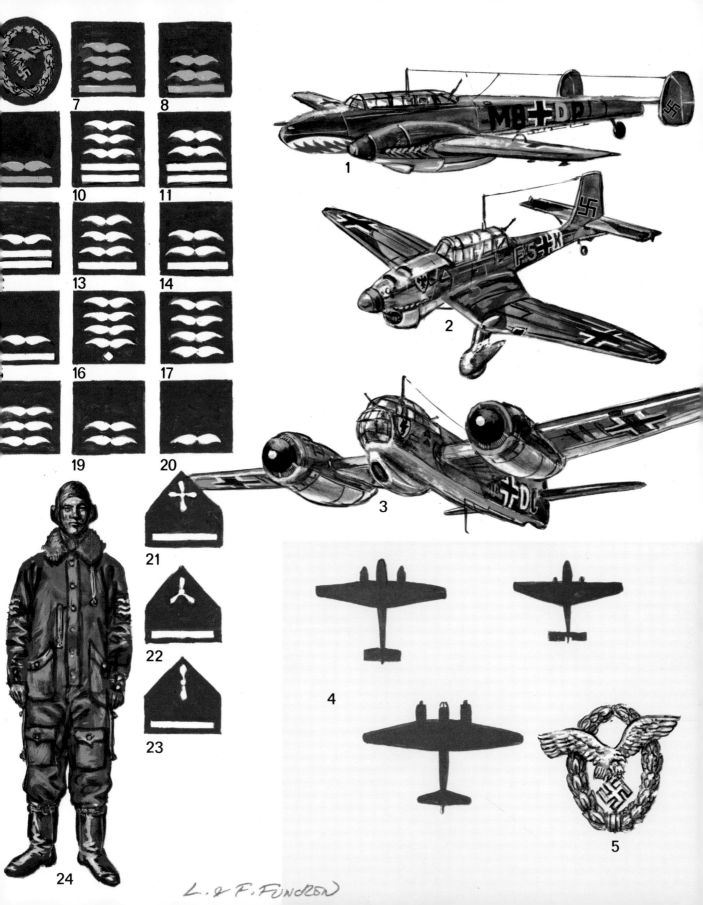

7

8

10

11

13

14

16

17

19

20

21

22

23

24

1

2

3

4

5

L. & F. FUNCKEN

PAINTWORK AND CAMOUFLAGE

The German aircraft rapidly developed a great variety of camouflage systems, that most often used on fighters consisting of large patches of dark green over a light green base. These patches had much more broken outlines than those of their opponents' aircraft, nor did they cover the sides of the fuselage, which were painted in different shades of light or mouse grey, often in patches of varying intensity. Certain fighter squadrons, such as the celebrated *Richthofen* squadron, sported a yellow nose and tail.

The use of unit emblems on the planes was very common and there was a great variety of designs, many of them humorous. As in the other air forces, these emblems had not been designed by professionals, and this amateur quality—particularly among the Germans—made them stand out in remarkable contrast from the admirably designed but sober emblems produced by official designers.

ORGANISATION

A *Staffel* (flight) consisted correctly of nine machines but in practice this number could go up to twenty. Three *Staffeln* made up a *Gruppe* and three *Gruppen* a *Geschwader*. The *Staffel* could be subdivided into *Schwärme* of four or five planes, *Ketten* of three planes, or *Rotten* of two planes.

UNIFORMS

The most important difference between the uniforms of the Luftwaffe and those of the other German forces was the basic colour, which in the Luftwaffe was grey-blue. The various uniforms and articles of attire used on different occasions were also much more varied. There was the *Tuchrock,* a tunic with revers resembling the *Feldbluse;* the special *Waffenrock;* the *Kleine Rock;* and the short *Fliegerbluse,* which was open at the neck and worn without a shirt beneath by soldiers and NCOs. The helmet carried the special Luftwaffe eagle on its left side.

THE 'WAFFENFARBEN'[1]

The different branches and services in the German air force were distinguished by the colour of the piping on their caps and by their shoulder straps, but mainly by their *Kragenspiegeln,* the rectangular patches decorating the collar.

Generals and the 'Regiment General Göring'	white
Flying personnel and paratroopers	yellow
Anti-aircraft artillery	red
General staff	carmine
Engineers	pink
Recalled officers[2]	orange
Signals	brown
Medical personnel	dark blue
Traffic controllers	light green
Administration	dark green
Air Ministry	black

1 The colours of the arms.
2 Reservist officers who have been recalled but who are still unattached.

GERMAN AIR FORCE, 1939-1941 IV

1. Heinkel 111 — 2. Dornier 17 — 3. Radio operator's insignia — 4. Officer's field cap — 5. Airman's field cap — 6–7. Soldier in field service dress — 8. Lieutenant in undress — 9. Officer, signals troops

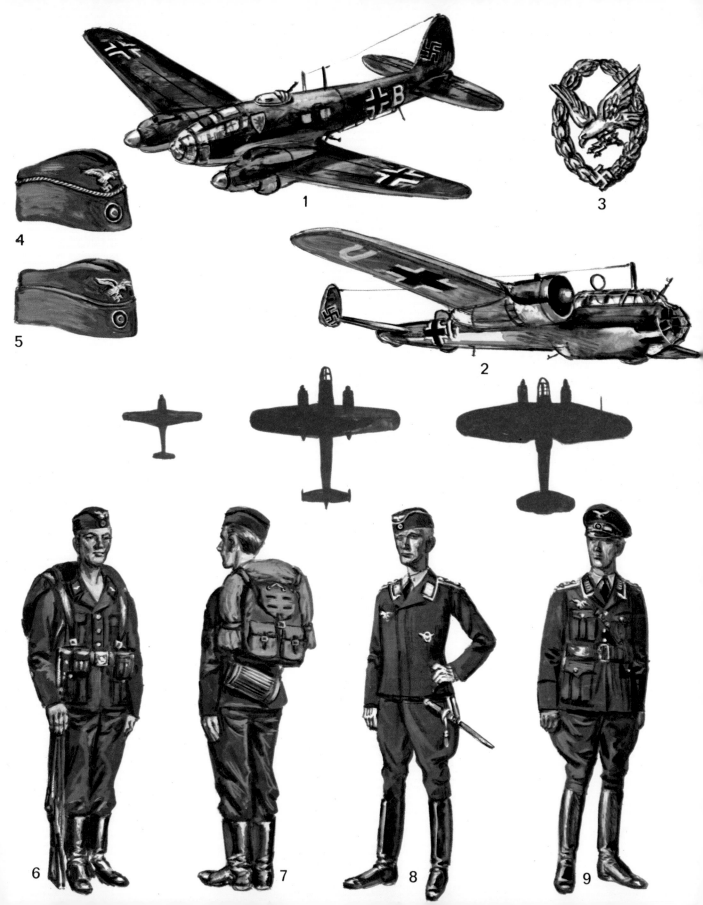

Comparison of Ranks in the Luftwaffe and the RAF

GENERAL OFFICERS	
Reichsmarschall	
General Feldmarschall	Marshal of the RAF
Generaloberst	Air Chief Marshal
General der Flieger	—
Generalleutnant	Air Marshal
Generalmajor	Air Vice-Marshal
SENIOR OFFICERS	
Oberst	Group Captain
Oberstleutnant	Wing Commander
Major	Squadron Leader
JUNIOR OFFICERS	
Hauptmann	Flight Lieutenant
Oberleutnant	Flying Officer
Leutnant	Pilot Officer
NON-COMMISSIONED OFFICERS	
Oberfähnrich	
Stabsfeldwebel	Warrant Officers
Oberfeldwebel	
Feldwebel	
Fähnrich	Flight Ensign
Unterfeldwebel	Flight Sergeant
Unteroffizier	Sergeant
JUNIOR NCOs AND MEN	
Hauptgefreite	Corporal
Obergefreite	Leading Aircraftman
Gefreite	Aircraftman 1st class
Flieger, Funker, Kanonier	Aircraftman 2nd class

PARACHUTE TROOPS

The 1st battalion of parachutists was inaugurated in 1936 and first appeared officially in the 1937 army manoeuvres. Drawn from General Göring's forces, the troops were made up entirely of regular soldiers. The army too had formed a parachute regiment, which quickly became a battalion, and these two battalions were brought together in 1938 under the general direction of the Luftwaffe. Brigadier Student, whose ideas about the instruction and deployment of parachute troops proved to be highly formative, was the officer in command.

During this initial period each battalion had a headquarters, a teaching section, three fighter companies and a heavy company. Each fighter company was made up of three groups subdivided further into three sections, each armed with eighteen light machine guns, three light mortars and three anti-tank guns. The heavy company had twelve heavy machine guns and six medium mortars.[1] Everyday uniform consisted of a short flying tunic with trousers tucked into specially designed shoes which rose high up the ankle. For jumping the paratroopers wore dungarees with short legs and zip pockets, the *Sonderbekleidung*, which was worn over the short flying tunic. The special helmet had no rim and was lined with rubber padding. Its weight was 1,450 grammes, some 150 grammes more than the standard Wehrmacht helmet. The parachute measured 54 square metres and was of the RZ1 and later of the RZ16 type.

FIRST CAMPAIGNS

Contrary to popular belief, the parachute troops played a considerable part in the Polish campaign, at the time of the crossing of the Bzura river. Subsequently they were involved in the operations in Denmark and Norway, followed by their extraordinary achievements at Eben-Emael[2] in Belgium, which was a prelude to the attack on Crete in 1941.

1 This structuring and arming went through numerous subsequent modifications (see pp. 84-6).
2 See vol. 1.

SOVIET AIR FORCE I

1. I.15 *bis* — 2. I.15 D — 3. I.16 — 4. I.16 (Spanish Civil War) — 5. I.17 — 6. Major-general, air force — 7. Cap and collar detail from fig. 6 — 8. Non-commissioned flying officer — 9. Cap and collar detail, fig. 8

The Soviet Air Force

One important part of the Soviet Union's Five Year Plan was the foundation of factories capable of producing a powerful air force for the country, and the most eminent Soviet scientists had been brought together to achieve this. They succeeded brilliantly, and today such names as Mikoyan and Gurevich (fathers of the Mig), and Yakovlev, Ilyushin, Lavochkin and Tupolev are famous throughout the world.

The first machine to attract specialist attention was the work of the elderly Nikolai N. Polikarpov. It was known by several different names: I.16[1] in Russia; *Mosca* (fly) or *Rata* (rat) in Spain, according to which side was using it; *Abu* (horsefly) by the Japanese who came up against it in China; and finally the Soviet pilots of 1941-2, who affectionately christened the indefatigable little plane *Ichak* (donkey). By 1941 the Polikarpov had long been out of date, but it was still there fighting at Stalingrad, this time using a special technique known as *taran*, which involved stripping the wings off enemy bombers with the aid of specially fitted steel propeller blades.

On its first appearance in battle in the Spanish skies, this little fighter was classified by world experts as one of those copies of foreign makes which the Soviet factories had been turning out. This assessment was false. The I.16 was the first monoplane to have low wings and a retractable undercarriage; it was also considerably faster than its rivals and was specially armoured to protect the pilot. Made in its thousands after 1933, this little fighter was to be outclassed by the Messerschmitt 109 during the Spanish Civil War, but yet it still withstood the main brunt of the Luftwaffe onslaught in 1941.

One of the first fighters to come to the rescue of the little I.16 was the Yak.1, designed by Alexander Sergeivich Yakovlev. This small fighter was to become the most celebrated of all the Russian planes in the Second World War and to beat all production records with its figure of thirty thousand machines. After its first tests it was named *Krasavec* (beauty) by the enthusiastic pilots, and its immediate success brought Yakovlev many honours and rewards, including the Order of Lenin, a *Zim* car, and a pension of a hundred thousand roubles. A few months later the title 'Doctor of Technical Science' was conferred on this amiable engineer, and finally he was decorated with the coveted 'Hero of the Socialist Worker'.

The Yak, however, was not to appear in Russian skies until the end of 1941, as the factories entrusted with its manufacture were either captured in the formidable German advance or at least threatened. New factories had to be built in Siberia and in the Urals, but these were erected with such energy that only three weeks after the arrival of the movable parts and tools the first Yaks were coming off the production line. Like many of its predecessors the new fighter was made almost completely of wood and plywood, covered with cloth and coated with a thick layer of varnish.

The Yak was to run through several versions,[2] each one methodically improving on the last, and the VVS-RKKA or *Voyenno-Vozdouchnye Sily Rabotcho-Krestyanskoi Krasnoi Armii* —'Red Army Workers' and Peasants' Air force'—was continually strengthened by the adoption of new planes, becoming a really impressive force. Among these new aircraft was the I.61 or Mig.A designed by Artion I. Mikoyan and Mikhail I. Gurevich, which passed from the drawing board to prototype stage in four months and made its début in the air force at the beginning of 1941. A little later it was rechristened the Mig.3, and under this name was to win a reputation which in later more sophisticated versions has lasted until the present day.

2 These and other types of aircraft will be described in vol. 4.

---

1 The 'I' standing for *Istrebitel* or fighter.

SOVIET AIR FORCE II

1. Il.2 two-seater — 2. Pe.2 — 3. Yak.1 — 4. Mig.1

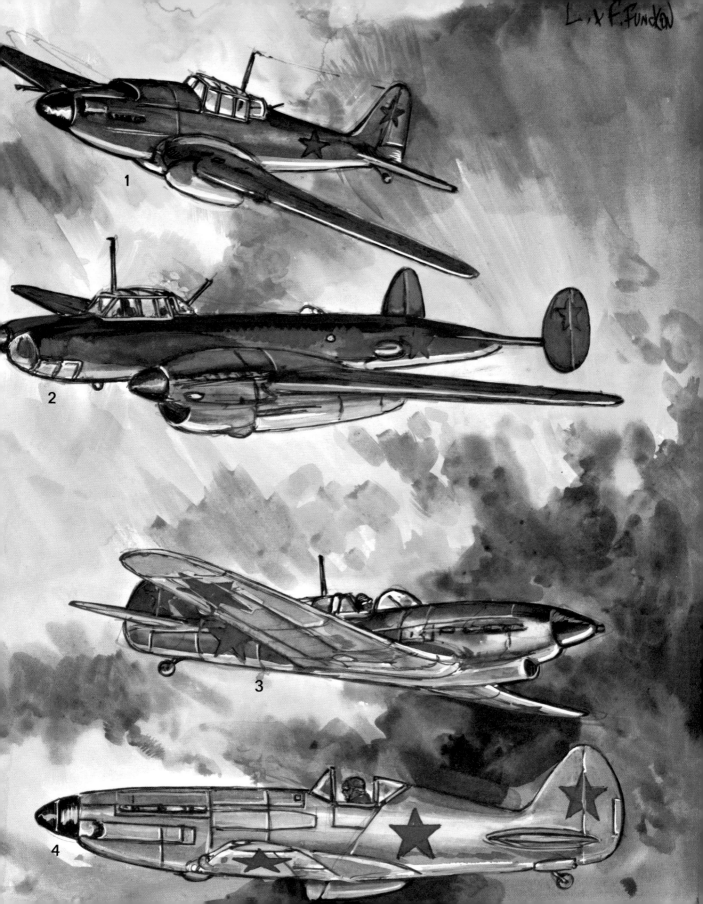

Another type of combat plane, the Il.2, designed by the engineer Sergei Vladimirovich Ilyushin, was to become famous as the *Shturmovik*, a name highly evocative of its fighting capacity. In fact, the two hundred and fifty Il.2s in existence in June 1941 were largely responsible for the few local victories pulled off by the Russians during the terrible first months of the invasion. The Soviet infantry christened these planes the 'infantry of the air', while to the Germans they were 'Iron Gustav' and then the 'Black Death'.

In the field of heavy bombers the Soviet Union was to make an equally formidable effort, but in 1941 modern machines such as the Pe.2 (designed by the engineer Vladimir Nikhailovich Petliakov, and an excellent dive bomber) were very rare, though the impressive Soviet industrial power was to increase their number rapidly from about five hundred for all fronts in 1941 to eleven thousand by 1945. The heavy DB.3, TB.3 and SB.2 bombers also played their part in the 'great patriotic war'

From the earliest days of that ferocious struggle—a sort of 'holy war', in which two fanatical ideologies came face to face—the Russians, outclassed on all sides, applied themselves to inflicting the maximum possible damage on the Germans with the still imperfect weapons they had at their disposal. Some pilots did not hesitate to hurl their half-destroyed machines on to the armoured German columns (one such being Captain N. F. Castello, in June 1941).

Some ingenious methods of attack were devised. Before the war, for example, the engineer Vakhmistrov had planned the use of huge four-engined machines to transport fighter planes. The first trial flights took place in 1935, with a Tupolev carrying five fighters, two on the wings, two below, and one beneath the fuselage. These short-range aircraft were only required to intervene to protect the bombers when they were over their target; then, their mission accomplished, they still had enough fuel to return to base. These experiments, which bordered on the eccentric and came to be nicknamed the 'Vackmistrov Circus', were pursued until 1940, but as an actual method of fighting the system was used only once during the war. In August 1941 a TB.3, loaded with two biplane fighter I.16s both carrying 250 kg bombs, released the fighters near a bridge over the Danube, which was known to be heavily defended by German anti-aircraft artillery. The two fighter bombers, whom no one could have expected to appear so far from their base, swooped down on the bridge and destroyed it before the anti-aircraft gun crews even had time to react. They then returned to base on their full fuel tanks, which of course had not been used before the beginning of the action.

The Pilots in Battle

The first months of the war proved as catastrophic for the Soviet aircrews as they had been for the other branches of the Russian forces. In one day alone, on the first of the 'Operation Barbarossa', twelve hundred aircraft were destroyed, many of them before they had had time to take to the air, so great had been the element of surprise in the German attack. The scorn with which the Nazis viewed the *Untermenschen,* the 'inferior races', of the east soon proved to be a costly error, underestimating as it did the tenacity and capacity of resistance of the Soviet masses.

The Soviet air force was organised into fighter, assault and bomber divisions, and came under military district commandants. From the beginning of the war it found itself battling under several

SOVIET AIR FORCE III

1. Tupolev TB.3 — 2. SB.2 — 3. DB.3F — 4. DB.3F and Me.109, comparison of outlines
5. Flying officer's uniform in 1938. Gradually this was replaced by the more usual colour — 6. Paratrooper with automatic rifle, the earliest Degtiarev of 1926

disadvantages. First of all, as we have already mentioned, it was badly outclassed by the German forces with regard to equipment. To this must be added the inexperience of the Russian officers and NCOs, faced with the revolutionary methods of the *Blitzkrieg*; and on top of this was the handicap of the army having been surprised in the middle of the extensive reorganisation to which we have already referred. The Red army had only one path left open to it—to close ranks and battle every inch of the way, destroying everything of any conceivable use before abandoning the territory to the enemy. In this unequal battle the Russian pilots sacrificed themselves unstintingly, and with a fierce will and self-denial only equalled by that of their brothers-in-arms on the ground below.

Women, who fought in considerable numbers in all the armed forces, were also present in the air. The first women pilots in the war had been recruited by Marina Raskova from the ranks of the supervisors of flying clubs and from students at the Institute in Moscow. It was a woman chemical engineer, Valerie Khomiakov, who pulled off the first air victory in the skies over Saratov. From more than twenty completely female fighter regiments, many aerial assault and bomber divisions were organised, and they fought with impressive efficiency from Stalingrad to Berlin.

PARACHUTE TROOPS

The Soviet Union was the first country in the world to organise parachute and airborne troops, which they had under way by 1935. In 1941 the Red army could muster some seven thousand parachute troops organised into seven brigades. These units did not take part in any large-scale war action but were utilised in small groups behind the enemy lines as saboteurs, radio operators and leaders of guerrilla groups.

The Belgian Air Force

In 1924 the Belgian air force was divided into three main groups, reconnaissance, fighting and bombing, which in 1928 gave rise to three regiments: the 1st air regiment was made up of machines designed for reconnaissance and observation, the 2nd for fighting, and the third for reconnaissance and bombing. At this time too the air force took the name *aéronautique militaire*—'military aerial navigation'—and adopted for its flying personnel the grey-blue uniform, with the flying 'A' on the left sleeve, from the First World War. The new uniform strongly resembled that of the RAF, both in colour and in its general appearance, but the Belgian cloth had slightly more grey in it.

In 1930 the re-equipment of the Belgian air force with machines of British manufacture began, but by the eve of the war it had become clear that the magnificent aircraft which had been purchased nearly ten years ago were now completely outclassed by the latest models in the air. It was decided to order ninety-five Hurricanes, but only eleven were actually received. Curtiss machines were also ordered from the United States, but France had first priority from the Americans and the Belgians were forced to fall back on the Brewster Buffalo; not a single one of all the machines ordered arrived in time. At the last moment Belgium decided to buy some Gladiators from Britain and thirty Fiat CR42s[1] from the Italians. These latter planes had been rejected five years earlier by the Belgian air force but necessity dictated that they now be bought.

1 CR stands for Celestino Rosatelli, Fiat's engineer-in-chief. Although a little out of date, the Fiat was nevertheless an excellent machine. Unfortunately it transpired that the cartridges delivered by Fascist Italy did not contain the necessary powder charge, and this caused serious failures during aerial battles.

BELGIAN AIR FORCE, 1939-1940 I

1. Renard — 2. Fairey-Fox — 3. Fairey-Firefly — 4. Gloster Gladiator — 5. Airman in walking-out dress

1

2

3

4

5

Lt & F. Puncken

On 10 May 1940 the Belgian air force numbered:
1st *regiment d'aéronautique militaire* (reconnaissance
and observation): six flights plus six aircraft in
reserve, making a total of sixty machines.
2nd *regiment d'aéronautique militaire* (fighters): six
flights plus six aircraft in reserve, sixty-two machines.
3rd *regiment d'aéronautique militaire* (reconnaissance and bombing): six flights plus six aircraft in
reserve, forty-one machines.

Modern machines in the force were fourteen
Fairey-Battles, twelve Hurricanes (of which one was
ex-British, seized in 1939 after a forced landing!),
thirty Fiats and thirteen Gladiators, making sixty-nine
aircraft out of a total of one hundred and eighty. The
10 May 1940 saw half this slender force destroyed in
the first fierce German onslaught, and most of those
lost were the more modern machines. Those which
managed to escape fought on with great courage,
harassed as they were by the swarms of Messerschmitt
109s and decimated by the terrible flak.[1] Twenty-nine
pilots lost their lives in this unequal battle, and
material losses rose to one hundred and fifteen
machines. Those pilots and navigators who escaped
fled to France with the last remaining planes, from
where they fought on until the Franco-German
armistice of June 1940. The majority then managed to
get to Britain, where they became an important
element in the ranks of the RAF for the rest of the
war.[2]

1 The German anti-aircraft artillery, the name being an
abbreviation of *Flugzeugabwehrkanone.*
2 From one hundred and twenty in August 1940, their numbers
reached eight hundred by 1944.

BELGIAN AIR FORCE, 1939-1940 II

1. Hurricane — 2. Fairey-Battle — 3. Fiat CR.42 — 4. Pilot
in flying dress

1

2

3

4

L·A·B·Funcken

PART THREE

GERMANY

The German Army from 1941 to 1943

In the previous volume we showed the standard light weapons used by the German infantry in the first campaign of the Second World War. Our object this time is to illustrate the modifications which were made to uniforms and weapons between 1941 and 1943. Nevertheless, in certain cases it will be necessary to go back to some types of weapons and details of equipment which found no place in the first volume of this work but which were, in fact, in use throughout the war.

GRENADE-THROWERS AND MORTARS

The Kampfpistole

This tiny grenade-launcher was based on the *Leuchtpistole,* which, as its name indicates, projected luminous flares or signal rockets but which after modification was capable of firing a much more dangerous projectile: either the 27 mm 326LP grenade, or the egg-shaped 361LP grenade of the traditional type propelled by a standard rocket. The weapon could therefore still be used as a simple signal pistol. Its range with the 326LP grenade was just under one hundred yards.

A later modification, known as the *Sturmpistole,* which was in effect an assault pistol with a folding shoulder-stock, could fire the formidable close-range hollow-charge projectiles.[1] Before this, the *Sturmpistole* fired four types of projectile: explosive, smoke, signal and parachute flare.

1 Hollow-charge projectiles are the subject of a chapter in vol. 4.

The 5 cm Granatwerfer 36

In effect a small mortar, this grenade-launcher wa introduced into service in 1936. It weighed nearly 31 lb but could be broken down into two parts fo transport purposes. The fact that it was fired by mean of a trigger distinguished it from the more tradition mortars from which the projectile was fired by its ow weight dropping on to the striker at the base of th tube.

This 5 cm grenade launcher was operated by two-man team, who lay flat on their stomachs, one o them holding the weapon still by grasping the two small handles mounted on either side of the base of th tube. The weapon could be elevated from an angle o 43° to 90° and the projectile had a maximum range o just under five hundred and fifty yards. The projectil was called the *Wurfgranate,* weighed a little over 2 lb and contained some $4\frac{1}{2}$ oz of TNT. It was painted dull red.

The 8 cm Granatwerfer 34

Complementing the *Granatwerfer* 36, the 8 cm GrW34 was a conventional medium mortar. It coul hurl an 8 cm *Wurfgranate* of the 34, 38 or 39 type weighing around $7\frac{1}{2}$ lb and containing just over 17 oz of TNT, some 2,620 yards. The colours of th projectiles were: chocolate brown for the Model 3 explosive grenade; dull red for the Model 34N smoke grenade; grey-green for the Model 3

GERMAN ARMY I

1. 5 cm Sturmpistole or Kampfpistole grenade-launcher – 2. 5 cm Granatwerfer 36 — 3. 8 cm Granatwerfer 34 — Nebelwerfer 35 for smoke bombs — 5. Kurzer Granatwerfe 42, a lightweight version of the 8 cm Granatwerfer 34 — Leichtes Infanteriegeschütz (LIG 18), 75 mm infantry h witzer

explosive grenade. The Allies nicknamed the Model 39 'Bouncing Betty'.

The weapon, together with its base and bipod support, weighed just over 123 lb; when carried on men's backs it could be broken down into three separate loads.

8 cm Kurzer Granatwerfer 42

Designed to combine the power of a medium mortar with the lesser weight of a light mortar, this short version of the 8 cm mortar was a scaled-down variant of the *Granatwerfer* 34 described above. It weighed only 62 lb but its range was reduced to about thirteen hundred yards.

The 10 cm Nebelwerfer 35

Literally a smoke or 'fog' projector, this heavy mortar was a bigger version of the 8 cm mortar and was originally intended for use by the pioneer troops to create smoke-screens with the help of the *Wurfgranate* 35. However, it was also used offensively with the Wgr 40 projectile, which weighed more than $15\frac{1}{2}$ lb and could be fired a distance of up to $2\frac{1}{4}$ miles. The projectile was grey-green in colour. The weapon itself weighed a little over 229 lb and could be moved about on a small two-wheeled carriage. It necessitated a five-man team.

The Nebelwerfer 40

This heavy 10 cm mortar was mounted on wheels and fired a bomb of the Wgr 40 type, weighing nearly 20 lb, up to $3\frac{3}{4}$ miles. The *Nebelwerfer* 40 weighed just over three-quarters of a ton.

The 12 cm Granatwerfer 42

In 1942 the Germans produced a mortar capable of offering some reply to the terrible blows inflicted by the Russian mortar of the same calibre. However, although it was rigidly based on the Russian model, the German Model 42 never seems to have quite matched up to it. Nevertheless, it was a formidable weapon, weighing nearly 613 lb, this being borne by a small two-wheeled carriage with pneumatic tyres. The bomb could be fired up to $3\frac{3}{4}$ miles.

At the beginning of the war the two principal mortars in use were the 5 cm Model 36 and the 8 cm Model 34. At that time, each infantry company was provided with three light mortars, while each machine gun company (of which there was one to each battalion) had as part of it a platoon carrying six 8 cm medium mortars. Towards 1942 the small 5 cm grenade-throwers were replaced by the new short 8 cm Model 42, which the troops nicknamed the *Stummelwerfer*, presumably because it reminded them of a short clay pipe. Unfortunately, this latest weapon, which had been intended to augment the fire-power of the infantry, was never quite in the same class as the formidable Soviet 12 cm mortar, and the *Stummelwerfer* was dropped when the new 12 cm mortar was introduced.

Those who have fought against the German army generally agree that it was an extremely unpleasant

GERMAN ARMY II

1. 7·92 mm MG 42 machine gun. It was very similar to the MG 34 (see vol. 1), although its stronger and shorter barrel enabled it to fire more powerful ammunition — 2. Machine gunners with the tripod for the heavy machine-gun version — 3. Method of firing employed by assault troops. The soldier carrying the barrel on his shoulders could turn his back to the enemy and thus move his head away from the muzzle — 4. 'Kleif' flamethrower, 1st Model — 5. Model 41, flamethrower

Special badges: 6. Wound badge. This was awarded in three classes: bronze, silver and gilt — 7. General assault badge — 8. Tank assault badge, awarded, up to June 1940, to members of tank units who distinguished themselves in three actions on three different days; the award was later extended to Panzergrenadiers, reconnaissance battalions, armoured car crews and medical personnel who accompanied the assaults — 9. After July 1943, as a more suitable reward for long service, a new type of tank assault badge was instituted for 25, 50, 75 or 100 assaults (in bronze, silver and gilt) — 10. Medal for the Winter Battle in the East 1941-42 (known as the 'Frozen Meat Order') — 11. Anti-partisan war badge — 12. Infantry assault badge (awarded for three assaults on three different days in the field against the enemy) — 13. Close combat clasp (for those who distinguished themselves in hand-to-hand fighting) — 14. Special badge for the single-handed destruction of a tank. This award was instituted in 1942 for soldiers who destroyed a tank or armoured car without the help of heavy anti-tank weapons. The badge was bronze on a silver background. Five of them could be worn, one above the other. In 1943 the same badge, but on a gold background, was instituted to symbolise five such victories. The grenadier in fig. 4 is wearing tank destruction badges on his right arm to indicate three such victories.

experience to be subjected to German mortar fire, because it was so intense and accurate. And indeed the astonishing skill of German mortar teams had already been recognised twenty-five years earlier.[1]

THE INFANTRY GUN

It is clear that in 1939 the German High Command felt that the enemy could be crushed by *Blitzkrieg* tactics, with tanks and aircraft operating together, rather than by the long preparatory artillery bombardments which had been typical of the First World War. As a result, the traditional artillery had only a secondary role to play, at least for a time. Nevertheless, the infantry was provided with a small support gun, the 7·5 cm *Leichtes Infanteriegeschütz* 18 (or light infantry gun), originally mounted on spoked wooden wheels and later on solid metal wheels with pneumatic tyres. Airborne troops were equipped with a lightweight version fitted with a shield. The gun weighed just under 900 lb and could be broken down into six loads, while its range was somewhat in excess of two miles.

There was also a mountain version of this small gun.

THE MASCHINENGEWEHR 42

This machine gun, the second and last in its category, was designed by Dr Grunow, an engineer in the firm of Johannes Grossfuss of Döbeln in Saxony. Judged to be one of the most remarkable machine guns ever made, the MG42 enjoyed, moreover, the enormous advantage of being much easier to manufacture than the MG34,[2] thanks to the adoption of revolutionary production methods, which for the first time in the history of world arms manufacture employed stamping, riveting and welding processes. The resulting benefits in terms of lower costs and ease of production were indeed considerable, but the saving in time was the most valuable benefit of all.

Like the MG34, the MG42 could serve as a light or as a heavy machine gun, according to whether it was mounted on a bipod or tripod. Its extremely high rate

1 See *Arms and Uniforms: The First World War.*
2 See vol. 1 of *The Second World War.*

of fire—nine hundred to twelve hundred rounds a minute—meant that it consumed ammunition greedily, while the overheating of the barrel necessitated more frequent changeovers than had been the case with the previous model; the MG42, apparently, was also less accurate than its predecessor. Be that as it may, this weapon acquired a reputation in the field which nobody thought of challenging. Although widely issued, the MG42 never completely supplanted the old MG34.

FLAMETHROWERS

The Model 35 flamethrower which was carried into the opening battles was based on the type used during the First World War. The fuel was contained in a tank with compressed nitrogen, and ignition was achieved by means of a hydrogen flame. This terrible weapon could spit ten jets of flame per second to a distance of just over thirty yards. However, the operator was severely restricted by the heavy tank, which weighed some 79 lb.

GERMAN ARMY III

1. The Zeltbahn or waterproof shelter triangle, here shown spread out — 2. Method of putting on the Zeltbahn — 3. The Zeltbahn worn loose (for marching) — 4. The Zeltbahn fastened between the legs to form semi-breeches for horse-riding (cavalry) — 5. The Zeltbahn worn tight around the thighs for cycle riding (cyclists) — 6. Two tent triangles used as a shelter from the wind — 7. Four shelter triangles joined together to form a tent measuring 2.40 metres square at the base and about 1.20 metres in height — 8. Alternative method of using two shelter tents as a wind-break. Helmet camouflage and methods of fastening: 9. Regulation issue camouflage cover — 10. With part of an inner tube from a motorcycle tyre — 11. Helmet covering made from a single piece of camouflage material — 12. Steel helmet coated with whitewash for fighting in snow-covered terrain — 13. Army issue canvas carrying straps attached to helmet to hold camouflage — 14. White cloth rag covering for snow camouflage, fastened by string — 15. With chicken wire mesh — 16. With barbed wire — 17. With sacking material — 18. Standard camouflage cover fastened with clips — 19. Standard helmet with leather strap, buckles and clips — 20. Helmet cover held in place with leather strap and spring clips — 21. Mountain cap (Bergmütze), with details of edelweiss badge and national eagle and cockade, worn by mountain light infantry troops — 22. Field cap (Einheitsfeldmütze) with special Jäger (light infantry or rifle unit) oak leaf insignia, introduced in August 1942

The Flammenwerfer Model 40

This portable flamethrower weighed only about 44 lb but this saving in weight was achieved at the expense of its fuel capacity, which was reduced by one-third.

The Flammenwerfer Model 41

Earlier flamethrowers had depended for their operation on two successive actions: first the fuel itself was projected, then it was ignited by a jet of burning hydrogen. By contrast, the 41 squirted out streams of petrol, which were immediately ignited by a simultaneous jet of hydrogen passing over an electric contact, which was situated at the end of the tube handled by the operator. By squeezing a trigger, the operator could project five jets of flame, which reached a temperature of 800° C. Although this particular model needed two cylinders, the saving in weight was appreciable, the whole flamethrower weighing only $37\frac{1}{2}$ lb.

The Flammenwerfer Model 42

This weapon was basically similar to the 41, but the fuel was ignited by means of 9 mm blank cartridges. With the same weight as the 41, it could project six 3-second jets of flame some thirty-five yards.

There was also a static flamethrower, which could be deployed from defensive fortifications. The weapons, called *Abwehrflammenwerfer,* looked like butane gas bottles to which a tube had been attached and then bent back horizontally. They could be operated electrically from a distance.

The portable flamethrowers were allotted at a ratio of six to each engineer battalion. A version on wheels and with bigger tanks was also issued, of which each battalion received three.

EQUIPMENT

In our first volume we described six types of lightweight equipment used by the Wehrmacht, and the reader will have noted the small roll of camouflaged cloth called the *Zeltbahn,* or waterproof shelter triangle. This ingenious piece of equipment was essential to the soldier in the field, serving him either as a poncho or as a tent quarter according to need.

Basically a waterproof cape, the *Zeltbahn* could be worn in various ways, as shown in the illustrations. When spread out, the cape formed an isosceles triangle, of which the base measured 2·40 metres and the sides 2·03 metres. A series of metal buttons, thirty-one to each side, allowed it to be fastened or folded in any way required. Each soldier carried two tent pegs plus a section of tent pole, thus permitting four men to make themselves a small pyramid-shaped tent which afforded shelter against the strongest winds and heaviest rain. In fact, the eight or sixteen-man tents were the most widely used.

The *Zeltbahn* was camouflaged according to the standard Wehrmacht or Waffen SS pattern; there was also a version which was predominantly green on one side and brown on the other.

Helmet Camouflage

In addition to the devices provided by the army, the German soldier often resorted to improvisation to solve his camouflage problems. One of the simplest methods relied on an elastic band cut from the inner tube of a motor-cycle tyre; when placed around the helmet, it served to hold in position tufts of grass or foliage. In muddy terrain the helmet could be given a coat of paint, then sprinkled with a mixture of earth and gravel, which would become encrusted on the paint, thus providing an excellent imitation of the immediate terrain. In winter, any shade of white, preferably whitewash, was used. It is interesting to note that some soldiers, clearly acting on patriotic motives, kept the national badge on the right side of

GERMAN ARMY IV

1. Early snow camouflage, using a sheet — 2. Camouflage snow apron. The reverse side was plain white — 3–4. Reversible parka or anorak worn by mountain troops — 5. Snowshirt — 6. Long white coverall coat for snow camouflage — 7. Two-piece snow suit with white jacket and trousers — 8. Single-piece snow overalls — 9. Sage-green windproof jacket worn by mountain troops — 10. Quilted undergarment for extremely cold weather — 11–12. Mouse-grey and white reversible parka, with matching overtrousers. When the white side was worn uppermost, coloured armbands were attached to buttons on the sleeves to help distinguish friendly from enemy troops.

1

2

3

4

5

6

7

8

9

10

11

12

&F.Funcken

their helmet. As will be seen in the illustrations, wire-mesh and barbed-wire were sometimes put to unexpected uses. After the Allied landings in Italy, camouflage netting taken from prisoners was extensively employed.

Camouflaged Clothing

Following the experiences of the first years of the war, it became clear that it was necessary to adopt clothing which was capable of rendering front-line troops less visible to enemy marksmen. A number of jackets and anoraks appeared, sometimes fur-lined but often reversible, and either camouflaged or in a single shade on one side and white on the other. Most are shown in the illustrations to this chapter.

The Russian campaign forced the Germans to adopt white clothing as soon as the first snowfalls occurred. Once again it became necessary to improvise and to commandeer, from the linen cupboards of Russian homes, all the bed sheets that could be found. Fixed on the helmet, the sheet hung down over the back, sometimes as far as the heels, making even the most ferocious warrior look something like a 'son of the desert' in an amateur theatrical production. The commissariat brought order to this welter of unorthodox garments as soon as they could by issuing the official *Heeres Tarnungskörperschürze* or camouflage body apron, which was camouflaged on one side and plain white on the other. This smock had only a limited life and soon had to give way to more suitable garments.

THREE SPECIAL FORMATIONS

The Panzergrenadiers

From November 1942 onwards all infantrymen were called *Grenadiere,*[1] while motorised infantry regiments and divisions accompanying the tanks took the name *Panzergrenadierregiment* or *Panzergrenadier-division.* The only distinguishing feature on the uniform was the *Waffenfarbe* or arm of service colour: apple green, in this case, on the collar and on the shoulder straps.

1 See vol. 1 of *The Second World War.*

The Feldgendarmerie

This body of military police formed an integral part of the German army. Its duties were those of all police forces of this type: traffic control, control duties at aerodromes, the rounding-up of stragglers, terrorists and deserters, the maintenance of discipline amongst German troops, etc.

The uniform worn by *Feldgendarmerie* personnel was the same as for the infantry with a few special but clearly visible badges alone indicating their function. First, there was the distinctive arm of service colour: in this case, orange on the collar and shoulder straps. Then there was the police-style eagle and swastika national emblem, surrounded by a wreath of oak leaves, the whole in orange and sewn on the left upper arm of tunic. Then came a brown cuff-title, bearing the word *Feldgendarmerie* embroidered in silver-grey and worn on the left forearm. Finally there was the remarkable gorget on which the name of the corps was repeated in luminous letters. The *Ringkragen* was also worn by a few other special formations, such as the railway station police or *Kommandantur* personnel; standard-bearers also wore them.

This *Ringkragen* or gorget was derived from an ancient piece of armour which covered the throat and chest but which, by the eighteenth century, had become so modified that it comprised no more than a crescent shape. The gorget disappeared in France around 1880; Germany had retained it but it was now

GERMAN ARMY V

1. Panzergrenadier — 2. Details of collar patch and shoulder strap with the distinctive soft apple-green colour — 3. Panzergrenadier with an ammunition box and a cylindrical carrying-case containing a spare machine-gun barrel — 4. Panzergrenadier from the crew of a reconnaissance vehicle, here dressed and equipped for fighting on foot — 5. Standard Bearer of a Pioneer regiment, with the gorget (*Ringkragen*), carrying sash and special armshield (worn on the right arm). The predominant colour on the armshield matched that of the standard — 6–8 Cavalry troopers — 9. Details of cavalry collar patch and shoulder strap — 10. Drummer — 11. 'Swallow's Nest': these were worn in matching pairs, one on each shoulder, by drummers and fife players (in this case of the artillery) — 12. 'Swallow's Nest' worn by regimental bandsmen (in this case of Jäger or light infantry and rifle units) — 13. 'Swallow's Nest' worn by drum-major (in this case of the air force, regiment of General Göring). The background colour is the same as the colour of the arm of service.

2

11

12

13

9

1

3

4

5

6

7

8

10

L. & F. FUNCKEN

worn hanging down over the chest, suspended from a flat-linked chain.[1]

In occupied countries the *Feldgendarmerie* had the additional duties of combating the 'black market', and hunting down rebels in collaboration with local police forces. It was also responsible for the transport and the supervision of detainees arrested by the *Geheime Feldpolizei* or the *Abwehr* (the secret military police and the counter-espionage service).

The Geheime Feldpolizei (Secret Field Police)

This military body was under the orders of a *Leitender Feldpolizeidirektor,* who worked in close cooperation with the *Abwehroffizier.* Although operating most frequently in plain clothes, the members of the *Geheime Feldpolizei* had a uniform similar to the normal army uniform but in a distinctive pale blue and with the letters GFP on the shoulder straps.

As for the formidable Gestapo or *Geheime Staatspolizei,* this was only one branch of the *Sicherheitspolizei-Sicherheitsdienst.* These were the State Secret Police and had no connection with the German army. We only mention them here so that the reader may grasp the essential—though barely apparent—differences which existed between it and other police forces.

1 The troops nicknamed the *Feldgendarmerie* 'the chained dogs'.

TODT ORGANISATION

1–2 Workers of the Todt Organisation wearing the field service uniform and greatcoat. (Note the 'Org. Todt' armband worn above the swastika armband)
Rank insignia worn on the collar and right arm: 3. Arbeiter — 4. Oberarbeiter — 5. Meister — 6. Obermeister — 7. Bauleiter — 8. Oberbauleiter — 9. Hauptbauleiter — 10. Einsatzleiter — 11. Einsatzgruppenleiter, 2nd Class — 12. Einsatzgruppenleiter, 1st Class — 13. Chef des Amtes Bau-OT
Special insignia worn on the left arm: 14. Bauführer — 15. Oberbauführer — 16. Hauptbauführer. The same badges indicated three types of Frontführer and doctors.

GERMAN WOMEN'S SERVICES

17. Luftwaffenhelferin, or Luftwaffe female auxiliary — 18. Riding school and horse-drawn transport auxiliary — 19. Nachrichtenhelferin des Heeres, or Army signals auxiliary. At the beginning of the occupation, the 'lightning-flash' badge worn on the field service cap and sleeve led to these

The Todt Organisation and the Women's Services

THE TODT ORGANISATION

Founded by the Nazi engineer Fritz Todt, this organisation's first task was to modernise the German road network, and it was due to the energetic direction of Todt himself that the first stretch of the Frankfurt-Darmstadt Autobahn was opened as early as May 1935. By 1938 this tireless engineer could pride himself on having laid down three thousand kilometres of the *Reichsautobahnen,* those dazzling 'symbols of the progress achieved by the Reich as a whole and by the dogged desire to work which characterised it under its Führer's leadership'.[2] Honours were heaped upon Todt, but his civil projects continued unabated until he was instructed to build the famous wall in the west, the *Westwall,* which in 1938 contained 6,000 bunkers and, by September 1939, some 13,700.

A year later the foundations of the Todt Organisation had been laid. This brought together, in para-military form, a whole legion of construction workers, which was to become one of the most important elements in Hitler's war machine. Following the lightning victory of 1940, the soldier-builders of the Todt Organisation went wherever the Wehrmacht fought, even building the Atlantic Wall,[3] of which one of the first concrete batteries was called the Todt Battery.

2 Edouard Schönleben, in *Fritz Todt,* 1943.
3 The *Westwall,* however, could not in any way be compared with the formidable Maginot Line.

auxiliaries being taken for 'SS Women'. Once this confusion had been cleared up, they were more simply nicknamed 'grey mice'
Ranks of Luftwaffenhelferinnen and Flakwaffenhelferinnen (Fig. 17 is wearing the special Flak or anti-aircraft artillery badge) 20. Helferin — 21. Oberhelferin — 22. Haupthelferin — 23. Führerin — 24. Oberführerin — 25. Hauptführerin — 26. Stabsführerin. These ranks correspond approximately to those ranging from Senior Private to Major. Before June 1941 they were symbolised by standard Luftwaffe insignia.

On 8 February 1942, at the age of fifty-one, the German 'master builder' was killed in an air accident. He was replaced by Reichsminister Albert Speer.

Uniform

The uniform of the Todt Organisation was brown, in a shade favoured by Nazi para-military units, while its badges were at first the same as those in use in the armed forces. It was not until 1 May 1943 that Speer authorised new insignia peculiar to the Todt Organisation. The different branches were distinguished by the background colour of the collar patches:

Construction workers	red
Administration	green
Works Direction	white
Music	black
Signals	yellow
Propaganda	brown
Medical	blue

An armband which bore the abbreviated legend 'ORG. TODT' was worn on the right arm above the swastika armband.

Junior personnel were not armed. Only the lorry drivers were issued with automatic pistols, or even sub-machine guns in less secure areas, most of which weapons were drawn from captured war booty often of Soviet origin.

To equip the volunteers recruited in the occupied countries, khaki uniforms captured in Belgium and France were widely used, with results which were both surprising and highly unorthodox.[1]

THE WOMEN'S SERVICES

The growing demands of the war led the Reich to recruit women for the auxiliary services as early as 1941. Mainly employed in offices or as telephonists,

[1] The reports of the activity of the Geheime Feldpolizei indicated serious lapses in discipline after 1941.

teletypists and even radio-operators, the 'grey mice',[2] as they were known, also served with the anti-aircraft defences. The highest rank was that of *Stabführerin* which roughly corresponded to that of company sergeant-major or warrant officer.

The Afrika Korps

For many readers the mere mention of the name of the Afrika Korps will be enough to remind them of the amazing exploits of this formation in the sands of North Africa, and there can be few who have not heard of Erwin Rommel, its dashing commander, who achieved the rare distinction of arousing the admiration of his most intractable enemies. Even Winston Churchill himself had to admit to a packed House of Commons: 'We have a very daring and skilful opponent against us, and, may I say across the havoc of war, a great general.'

The real significance of all these tributes can be better appreciated if one remembers that the saga of the Afrika Korps was written by only two thin armoured divisions, the 15th and 21st, and a makeshift light division, the 90th. The only reinforcement which Hitler deigned to send to this 'secondary' front was an infantry division. One must not forget, however, that eight Italian divisions were present in this theatre of operations, which, although they were poorly armed and equipped, did what they could in this merciless battle.

[2] The nickname given by the French and Belgians.

GERMAN ARMY, AFRIKA KORPS

1. Original standard tropical field service dress — 2. Same, seen from the back, with haversack or field pack — 3. Officer — 4. Engineer (other ranks) dressed in lightweight khaki drill — 5. Motorcyclists — 6. With tropical field service jacket and trousers — 7. With winter tunic and special ammunition pouches for Schmeisser sub-machine gun magazines — 8–9. Cloth field service cap (Feldmütze) and field cap (Einheitsfeldmütze) — 10. Tropical or 'Colonial' sun helmet — 11. Steel helmet — 12. Field cap in light drill material

L. & F. Funcken

UNIFORMS

Although the glory of the Afrika Korps has remained undiminished, details of their uniforms seem less fresh in people's minds. The standard tropical field service jacket with patch pockets is generally described as being of a light olive-green colour, which became bleached in the blazing sun into a light greenish tan. A report contained in *Der Standhafte Zinnsoldat* for June 1942, however, describes the colour as '*sattes Olivgrün*', i.e. a dark olive-green, and an example of the field service jacket in question, which is preserved in the showcases of the Army Museum in Brussels, is of precisely that colour. However, it is a fact that the dye did not stand up for long to the scorching sun and, as the reliable source quoted above says, soon turned into a light olive-grey.

The light field caps, of the type worn by mountain troops, were bleached almost white by the sun, and all the other articles of clothing suffered a similar change. The fine tropical sun helmet appears to have been quickly abandoned, the majority of photographs taken at the time showing the field cap or steel helmet being worn. The riding breeches also rapidly disappeared, as did the canvas and leather high lace-up tropical boots.

Luftwaffe personnel wore uniforms of the same cut as those of other arms, although they were made of a much lighter fabric: the colour was a light yellow ochre tinged with brown.

Straight trousers, worn outside the boots, and shorts also appeared. The greatcoat, initially olive-green, then of the standard continental field-grey type, was also in service, but this article of clothing did not of course suffer from the same degree of fading as it was normally only worn during bad weather or through the cool night hours.

After the capture of Tobruk, and the more difficult capture of Bir-Hacheim, which had been held by a tiny brigade of the Free French, the body-blow of El Alamein marked the end of the series of victories achieved by the Afrika Korps over a fifteen-month period, from March 1941 to June 1942. It seemed as if the gods of war had changed sides. Montgomery forced Rommel into a memorable retreat of some two thousand miles, which drove the enemy back to the sea

and ended in the last battle of the Afrika Korps: the Battle of Tunis on 19 April 1943. A month later nearly three hundred thousand Germans and Italians laid down their arms, crushed by the Anglo-American forces and the Free French units of Larminat and Leclerc, which now outnumbered the Axis units in aircraft and tanks by six to one. Field-Marshal Rommel, who had been evacuated two months earlier following a violent attack of malaria, thus escaped from his conquerors only to meet death by enforced suicide on 14 October 1944.

The Parachute Forces

After their spectacular performance on the Western Front in 1940 the German parachute troops next participated in the campaign in Greece, and it was as a result of their decisive intervention at the Corinth Canal that the German forces were able to drive rapidly into the Southern Peloponnese.

The next stage in the conquest, however, the attack on the island of Crete, was to be a quite different affair, for this time their opponents did not let themselves be taken by surprise. Greeted by a storm of lethal fire, the first glider formations landed in some disorder, some crashing and some even coming down in the middle

GERMAN PARACHUTE FORCES

1. Basic combat equipment — 2. With the Sturmgepäck (assault pack) — 3. In camouflaged smock and ammunition bandolier — 4. Complete combat equipment (Crete) — 5. With life-jacket and knee protectors (Crete) — 6. With shorts (Crete) — 7. Hybrid equipment (Italy) — 8. In tropical jacket and trousers (Italy) — 9. General (Crete) — 10. Summer shirt and trousers (Italy) — 11. Special gravity-blade knife — 12. Helmet for summer campaigns — 13. Helmet with captured camouflage net — 14. Helmet with standard camouflage cover — 15. Fallschirmjägergewehr 42/44 automatic rifle designed for parachute troops — 16. Model 42. These almost identical automatic rifles, which were both of 7.92 mm calibre, had elevated sights and folding bipods. They could also be fitted with telescopic sights. Even with the bayonet extended they were only a little over 3 foot in length.

of British positions. Initially, too, the parachute battalions fared no better: the 3rd Battalion was almost totally wiped out before it reached the ground; the 3rd Medical Company lost many men when it landed in the middle of Crete's olive groves; and one section of the 2nd Battalion lost thirty-seven out of forty men, slaughtered by partisans. Even more devastating was the fact that many paratroops of the second wave had been drowned in the sea when they had been dropped prematurely.

On the ground the fighting was extremely bitter, particularly where the paratroops came up against the New Zealanders, those crack troops of the British Empire. Scattered and often leaderless, the paratroops had to cope with desperate situations from which they managed to extricate themselves only by considerable initiative and an overwhelming will to win.

Thanks to many examples of outstanding heroism, and to reinforcement by mountain troops, who were brought in by the Ju.52 transports,[1] victory finally smiled upon the invaders. Among their number was a highly unorthodox parachutist, Colonel Ramcke, who, caught out by a sudden change of orders, had jumped in riding boots and breeches!

Paradoxically, the conquest of Crete in nine days by 23,464 German troops against 32,000 British, 15,000 Greeks and more than 10,000 partisans, at the cost of 3,986 killed or missing,[2] led only to the abandonment of this type of operation. Instead, it was left to the Allies to exploit more fully the possibilities demonstrated by General Student's parachute forces.

The last major parachute drop was on the bridges across the Dvina, on the Baltic. In North Africa, a combined German and Italian commando-type operation against the Allied supply lines met with partial defeat in 1943. The last three German airborne operations of any significance were the rescue of Mussolini from the Abruzzi in September 1943; the unsuccessful attempt to kidnap Marshal Tito, in May 1944, from his hideout at Drvar in Bosnia; and, finally, the dropping of von der Heyde's battle group behind the Allied lines in the Ardennes in December 1944.

Organised into divisions from 1943, the paratroops henceforth fought as orthodox infantry in the Balkans (1st Division in 1943), in the Ukraine (2nd Division in 1943-4) and, above all, in Italy (1st, 2nd and 4th Divisions) and France (2nd, 3rd, 5th and 6th Divisions). The last five divisions, numbered from 7 to 11, fought in Holland and to the very end in the defence of the Reich alongside the remnants of the older divisions.

At the outset of hostilities these divisions contained three parachute regiments, one artillery regiment, one armoured group, one anti-aircraft group, one pioneer battalion, one signals group, and a number of supply units. However, from 1944 onwards the divisions saw their strength whittled away, and the remains of other divisions were then amalgamated with them.

The story of the 'Green Devils' will always be firmly linked with the Battle of Monte Cassino, particularly in the case of the six survivors of the 7th Company of the 3rd Regiment, who only abandoned the enormous mass of ruins when all their ammunition was gone.

One could perhaps accuse the defenders of Monte Cassino of being Nazi fanatics, and indeed since they first went to school these young soldiers had been subjected to intensive propaganda to fill them with National Socialist ideals. But it would perhaps be fairer to ascribe their bravery to their comradeship, *esprit de corps,* and fighting qualities, which led them to do their duty. Certainly, it was these very qualities which helped the French and Anglo-American airborne forces to carry out the daring operations which adorn *their* annals.

GERMAN ARMY, RUSSIAN AUXILIARY TROOPS

1. Officer of the Vlasov Army — 2. Terek Cossack — 3. Don Cossack — 4. Russian Army of Liberation, other ranks Ranks of the Vlasov Army (shoulder straps): 5. General — 6. Colonel — 7. Lieutenant-Colonel — 8. Major — 9. Captain — 10. Lieutenant — 11. Second Lieutenant — 12. Company Sergeant-Major — 13. Sergeant-Major — 14. Sergeant — 15. Corporal
Arm insignia: 16. Turkistan, first pattern (from 1942 to 1945) — 17. As above, second pattern (little used, mid-1943) — 18. Same, third model (rare, end of 1943). National cockade worn on the field service cap — 19. Azerbaidzhan, with field service cap cockade — 20–21. Vlasov Army, with cockade — 22 and 27. Ukraine — 23. Kuban Cossacks — 24. Terek Cossacks — 25. Don Cossacks — 26 Siberian Cossacks

---

1 Three thousand Italian troops landed in the Bay of Sitia on 28 May, but they played only a small part in the capture of the island.
2 Including the losses of the Luftwaffe.

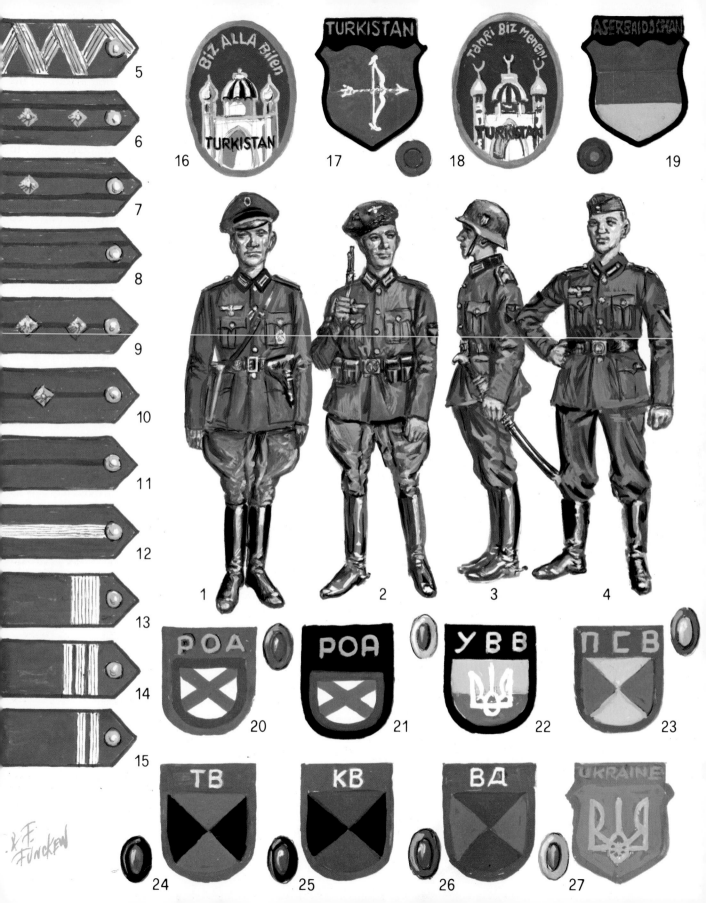

5

6

7

8

9

10

11

12

13

14

15

16 BIZ ALLA Bilen TURKISTAN

17 TURKISTAN

18 TaṅRi Biz Menen TURKISTAN

19 ASERBAIDSCHAN

1

2

3

4

20 POA

21 POA

22 УВВ

23 ПСВ

24 ТВ

25 КВ

26 ВД

27 UKRAINE

The Russian Volunteers

Of all the legions of volunteers raised for the fight against Bolshevism, the most numerous were those furnished by many of the former Soviet peoples following their 'liberation' by the German forces. Some of these volunteers joined up for political reasons, hoping thereby to obtain—after the victory, which now seemed to be approaching fast—some measure of self-government for the defunct Soviet republic from which they had come. The majority of the legionnaires, however, were undoubtedly motivated by less elevated ideals. Whether deserters or turncoats, prisoners of war or common law prisoners, they were concerned only with getting enough to eat, and eagerly seized the opportunity which was presented to them.

The German military authorities, under no illusions from the beginning, quickly became aware of the doubtful military value of these disturbing cohorts; they never entrusted them with anything more than minor tasks, one such being the struggle against the Soviet partisans, who with growing daring began to appear in increasing numbers behind the Wehrmacht's lines.

Some units, however, escaped this well merited contempt; one such was made up of the superb horsemen of the 15th Cossack Cavalry Corps, in which genuine Don and Kuban Cossacks were grouped together under the authority of German officers. Nor could there be any doubts about the nine White Russian battalions from Byelorussia, or White Russia—one of the republics of the Soviet Union before the German invasion. In fact the members of this White Russian Defence Corps were granted the honour of being allowed to fight at the front and, in 1944, of being admitted to the ranks of the Waffen SS.

Two other peoples, the Estonians and the Latvians, only recently annexed by the Soviet Union, lined up alongside the Germans. These Baltic peoples too enjoyed the confidence of their new masters and fought with vigour in the East, both in the battalions of the Legion and in the ranks of the Waffen SS. For a time they wore their own national uniforms before being clothed in the uniform of the Wehrmacht. The Lithuanians as well enthusiastically followed the lead of their Estonian and Latvian neighbours, inspired by the same feelings of bitterness towards their former conquerors.

In the case of the authentic Russian peoples, who even so presented a mosaic of the most diverse races, their units were at first employed on the spot in the battle against the partisans. Then, once the Soviet counter-offensive had been unleashed, they were disbanded, reorganised into larger formations, and sent to distant occupied territories such as Yugoslavia, Italy and France. Some legions, however, retained their own personality, like the one from Turkistan, and that of the turncoat General Vlasov, whose legion became by far the most famous of all the legions raised in Russia.

The 'Vlasov Army' undoubtedly owed its fame to the intense publicity given to it by the Nazi propaganda machine, which called for a mass uprising of peoples in the occupied territories for the 'crusade against Bolshevism'. Its long stay in France only added to its unhappy reputation, although this particular formation was certainly not the first of its kind to have been created, and was a long way from being the most important. Virtually an instrument of propaganda, the Vlasov Legion only became truly operational in 1944, under the name of the Russian Liberation Army or POA. It fought against the French Resistance and the Allied invasion forces in Normandy, then went on to fight in Czechoslovakia, first against the partisans

GERMAN ARMY, RUSSIAN VOLUNTEERS

1. Cossack of the 'Plato' regiment — 2. Don Cossack wearing the traditional *bachlyk* or hooded cloak — 3. Russian Army of Liberation (other ranks) — 4. Terek Cossack, dressed for winter sentry duty. Both 3 and 4 are wearing captured uniforms of unknown origin — 5 to 20. Arm insignia: 8. Kalmucks — 9. Volga Tartars — 10. Crimean Tartars — 11. Ukraine, variant (see preceding plate) — 12. Vlasov Army, first pattern
21. Ranks of the Russian Army of Liberation (shoulder straps) beginning, at top left, with the rank of Private, then as for the Vlasov Army as illustrated on the previous page, except for the rank of Company Sergeant-Major — 22. Collar insignia (collar patches) for other ranks and officers — 23. As above for units attached to the Wehrmacht — 24. Cossack rank insignia, as for the Vlasov Army, apart from three classes of General Officers (the last three gold embroidered badges to the right)

DON 5

RUSSLAND 6

ARMENIEN 7

8

9

10

УВВ 11

12

21

22   23

TEREK 13

BERGKAUKASIEN 14

IDEL-URAL 15

KUBAN 16

GEORGIEN 17

IDEL-URAL 18

ASERBAIDSHAN 19

ARMENIEN 20

1   2   3   4

L.v.& F. Funcken

24

and then with them. They ended up as prisoners, some captured by the Russians and others by the Americans.

The last of Vlasov's mercenaries, who were incarcerated in France, ended their career in wretched style when they were used as bargaining counters in an exchange for French SS prisoners of the Soviet Union. The other legionnaires of Russian origin probably met the same fate, apart from a few isolated groups who became the victims of lynch-mobs, as at Poitiers, or who were hunted down in the areas of their main exploits by the Maquis of the Ariège and other regions.

UNIFORMS

The most widely used uniform was that of the Wehrmacht, with a distinguishing feature in the form of a national badge on the right arm, or in the case of the POA and Cossacks on the left arm. Numerous photographs, however, reveal that in practice there was an almost total lack of such insignia. They also show how inventiveness ran wild in many units. For example, in one photograph depicting five officers of the 3rd Kuban Regiment, five different types of headgear can be seen, including a grey astrakhan fur cap stretched wider at the top in the Cossack style; a similar cap in black; a cylindrical grey astrakhan cap; a flat Russian peaked cap; and an unmodified flat German peaked cap. While the uniforms are identical and typically German, apart from the high boots, the collar patches are all different and constitute a real challenge to the armchair experts on uniforms and dress regulations. The insignia of POA units attached to the Wehrmacht can be seen side by side with the German *Litzen*—when these badges are not totally absent.

When off duty, these same Cossacks were permitted to wear their long black kaftans, lined with scarlet, or even the *bachlyk,* the hooded shawl with a tassel and coloured braiding.

It is evident that stricter rules were applied in the larger infantry formations, but even in this case it is dangerous to generalise, for here too strange uniforms were to be found, undoubtedly as a result of sheer necessity, such as the Dutch uniforms from 1940, which bore little relation to the German uniform.

Individual arms and equipment were subject to the same variations, although more often than not these were taken from the huge stocks of weapons captured from the Red army during the opening months of 'Barbarossa'.

The Russian legions brought with them their own form of transport, the curious little horse-drawn vehicles of the Russian peasants. Horses were also exported: small, shaggy and broad-backed, they had a legendary capacity for endurance which went back to the days of Genghis Khan. An amazing adventure, which happened to one of them in Belgium, fully supports this assertion, although one suspects that the story has been somewhat exaggerated in the re-telling. During the severe winter of 1943-4, a horse belonging to a detachment of the Turkistan Legion slipped into the icy waters of the Willebroek Canal. As it was getting dark, the troops postponed the rescue attempt until the following day and contented themselves with keeping the wretched animal's head above water by means of a halter fixed to a stake. The next morning the beast was hauled on to the bank, as stiff as a board and seemingly lifeless; a few minutes later, after a number of kicks accompanied by impatient shouts, the little horse got up and trotted off towards its feed. The finest tales often contain more than a grain of truth!

GERMAN ARMY, WAFFEN SS I

1. Other ranks, 1939-40 — 2. NCO, 1940 — 3. Officer — 4. General Officer in greatcoat — 5. Field service cap (Feldmütze), first pattern, 1934 — 6. Detail of the stamped metal death's head badge (SS-VT) — 7. Second pattern field service cap, worn until mid-1940 — 8. Detail of the eagle — 9. Field service cap worn from 1940 to 1942. The chevron with the arm of service colour disappeared in 1942 — 10. Detail of the embroidered or woven death's head badge (in metal on the peaked uniform cap or Schirmmütze) — 11. Final pattern of the field service cap — 12. Detail of the eagle — 13. The standard officer's peaked cap (Schirmmütze) — 14. NCO's peaked cap — 15. Old model peaked cap, dropped in 1942, but worn here by SS Hauptsturmführer Michael Wittmann with the black Panzer uniform, an additional twist to the regulations. This remarkable tank commander, who was killed in Normandy in 1944, was credited with a record of 138 tanks and 132 anti-tank guns destroyed in combat.

1

2

5

6

7

8

9

10

11

12

3

4

13

14

15

L.&F.FUNCKEN

The Waffen SS

In the first volume of this work, we spoke about the general SS and its first purely military offshoots, the SS-VT or *SS-Verfügungstruppen* (Armed Reserve Troops). In March 1940 these élite troops were collectively given the name of Waffen SS ('Armed SS') by order of their chief, Himmler, the title being officially ratified by Hitler the following July.

Up to May 1940, the first three *Standarten* or regiments of the SS-VT, *Deutschland, Germania* and *Der Führer,* had fought together at the heart of the first SS-VT division, which also contained an engineer battalion, a signals battalion, two reconnaissance companies, an anti-tank detachment and an anti-aircraft machine-gun battalion. Continually strengthened in the following months, the 1st VT division was re-christened *SS Division Reich* on 22 October 1940. From the same date the terms *Standarte, Sturmbann, Sturm* and *Zug* ceased to exist as designations of the regiment, battalion, company and platoon respectively, and henceforth the terminology used throughout the Wehrmacht was adopted, i.e. *Regiment, Bataillon,* etc.

The command of the 1st SS Division was entrusted to Paul Hausser, who can truly be considered the 'Father of the Waffen SS'. It was this former lieutenant-general of the by now defunct Reichswehr who had established the first SS officers' training school in 1934. Two years later given the title of inspector-general of the SS-VT, he was hero-worshipped by his men. He remained in this post until 1 October 1941 when he was promoted to the rank of SS Obergruppenführer and subsequently placed in command of the SS Panzer Korps.

In April 1941 the *Reich* Division assumed the divisional title *Das Reich* and became No. 2 in the list of divisions. There were eventually to be thirty-eight of them, of which the main features are summarised in the following pages.

The real 'champions' of the Third Reich, the large, purely German divisions of the Waffen SS, always fought with an extraordinary tenacity which led them to suffer enormous losses, finally reaching 50 per cent of their effective strength. Immediately after them came the French, Walloons, Flemings, Dutch and Scandinavians, though not everyone in this mass of three hundred thousand foreign SS troops demonstrated the same grim courage.

One hundred and forty thousand strong in 1942, the Waffen SS numbered three hundred thousand men by 1943 and six hundred thousand by 1944-5, an increase which was achieved not only by drawing upon the annual quota of conscripts and by recruiting members of the Hitler Youth who were under eighteen, but also—and mainly—by enlisting an improbable collection of different ethnic types who were much less committed to Nazi ideals. In the end, these 'outside' recruits were to comprise nearly half of the effective manpower of the Waffen SS. To illustrate this catholicity, out of a hundred possible examples, one is the recruiting campaign conducted in 1944 in the camps for deported workers by Léon Degrelle, commander of the 28th SS Panzer Grenadier Division 'Wallonie'. However, it achieved only meagre results, bringing in recruits whose only aim was to escape from vermin and hunger.

GERMAN ARMY, WAFFEN SS II

1. Bergmütze or mountain cap worn by SS mountain troops, with its edelweiss badge — 2–3. 1943 pattern field cap (Einheitsfeldmütze), inspired by the Austrian field cap of 1914-1918. Seen here are models with one and two buttons. Fig. 3 shows the silver or aluminium piping for officers around the crown — 4. Camouflaged model 1943 field cap. Before this period, it was worn without insignia (from June to December 1942). All these caps of the new pattern bore the designation Einheitsfeldmütze or General issue field cap, and were intended to replace the field service cap or Feldmütze — 5. SS steel helmet showing the SS runes on a silver shield, as worn on the right side, with (below) the national red shield with white circle and swastika as worn on the left side — 6. Steel helmet worn by SS Police units, showing the police badge worn on the left side. On the right side were the SS runes and shield as shown in fig. 5 — 7. Leather face mask for winter use, with the Russian-type fur cap which could show only the SS Totenkopf or death's head emblem. This face mask was generally reserved for anti-aircraft gunners and machine gunners on armoured vehicles and trains, who were exposed to the icy winds of the Russian Steppes — 8. Tropical sun helmet worn in southern regions of Europe, with insignia — 9. SS paratrooper's helmet, worn with or without the Luftwaffe eagle. No insignia on the right side — 10. Standard assault dress and equipment — 11. Camouflaged smock — 12. Complete camouflage suit, including face mask and gloves, as worn by crack marksmen or snipers in advanced outposts

NUMBER AND NAME	COLLAR PATCH	CUFF TITLE	HISTORY
1st SS Panzer Division 'Leibstandarte Adolf Hitler'	SS runes [1] ('LAH' monogram on shoulder straps)	Adolf Hitler	Motorised division in 1939. Poland 1939, then France 1940. Panzer Division in 1942, Russia. Italy in 1943. Russia and France in 1944. Ardennes offensive in 1944, then Germany.
2nd SS Panzer Division 'Das Reich'	SS runes (Shoulder strap insignia: D = Deutschland DF = Der Führer)	Das Reich	Panzer-Grenadier Division in 1941, Balkans, Russia, France in 1942. Then Russia from 1942 to 1944 and Ardennes in 1944. Germany, Hungary and Slovakia 1945.
3rd SS Panzer Division 'Totenkopf'	Death's head	Totenkopf	Formed in 1939, Poland. France in 1940. Russia in 1941 and 1942. France then Russia in 1943-44. Poland in 1944, then Hungary and Austria in 1945.
4th SS-Polizei Panzer-Grenadier Division	SS runes	SS Polizeidivision	Formed in 1939, Poland. France in 1940. Russia in 1941. In 1943 Bohemia-Moravia and Poland. Yugoslavia and Greece in 1944. Prussia then Berlin in 1945.
5th SS Panzer-Grenadier Division 'Wiking'	SS runes	Wiking Germania Westland Nordland	Formed in 1940 from Dutch, Danes, Flemings, Norwegians, Finns, Estonians. Russia 1941-44, then Poland, Hungary. Czechoslovakia in 1945.
6th SS Gebirgs Division (Mountain Division) 'Nord'	SS runes	Nord Reinhard Heydrich Michael Gaissmar	Formed in 1941. Finland until 1944, then Ardennes and Germany in 1945.
7th Freiwilligen Gebirgs Division (Mountain Div.) 'Prinz Eugen'	Special Rune [2] (The Odal Rune)	Prinz Eugen	Formed in 1942 from Serbs and Rumanians of German stock. Montenegro, Croatia in 1942-43. Italy in 1943. Bosnia in 1944, then in Yugoslavia until 1945.
8th SS Kavallerie Division (Cavalry Div.) 'Florian Geyer'	SS runes	Florian Geyer	Formed in 1942. Balkans, Czechoslovakia and Hungary until 1945.
9th SS Panzer Division 'Hohenstaufen'	SS runes	Hohenstaufen	Formed in 1942. Poland, France. In 1944: Russia, then France, Holland and Ardennes. Hungary in 1945.
10th SS Panzer Division 'Frundsberg'	SS runes	Frundsberg	Formed in 1942. France, then Russia in 1944. Subsequently, France in 1944 and Holland. Germany in 1945.

1 Characters of the ancient Germanic and Scandinavian alphabets.
2 See vol. 1, page 63, fig. 16.

GERMAN ARMY, WAFFEN SS III

1. Helmet painted with whitewash for winter camouflage — 2. As above, with SS runes visible. Here the paint has been mixed with earth from the surrounding terrain — 3. Helmet with spring camouflage cover — 4. 'Brick and plaster' camouflage helmet cover for urban fighting — 5 to 9. Examples of variations in camouflage patterns according to the season and types of surrounding vegetation — 10. Dutch volunteer of the SS Legion 'Nederland', 1941. The national shield was worn on the upper arm or forearm. The helmet shield was worn only for a time — 11. Member of the Italian SS. The armshield could have either vertical or horizontal stripes. The sleeve eagle could be embroidered on a black or red background and gripped a fasces in its talons (see right). The right collar patch could bear a silver Lictor's fasces emblem — Arm insignia: 12. Norway — 13. Croatia — 14. Galicia — 15. Latvia — 16. Estonia — 17. Albania — 18. Belgium (Walloon) — 19. France — 20. Flanders (Flemish) — 21. Holland — 22. Finland — 23. Italy (variation)

1

2

3

4

5

6

7

8

9

10

11

12

13

14

15

LATVIJA

16

17

18

19

WALLONIE

20

21

22

23

L. & F. FUNCKEN

NUMBER AND NAME	COLLAR PATCH	CUFF TITLE	HISTORY
11th SS Freiwilligen Panzer-Grenadier Div. 'Nordland'	Circular swastika or Danish 'solar wheel'	Danmark Freikorps Danmark Norge Hermann von Salza	Formed in 1943 from Dutch, Danish and Norwegian volunteers. In 1943, Croatia then Russia. Berlin in 1945.
12th SS Panzer Division 'Hitler Jugend'	SS runes	Hitler Jugend	Formed in 1943. Belgium then Normandy (1944) and Ardennes. Austria in 1945.
13th Waffen Gebirgs Division der SS 'Handschar', Kroatisches No. 1 (Croatian No. 1)	Swastika and scimitar	—	Formed in 1943 from Croatian volunteers. Mutinied in France, then sent to the Balkans. Disbanded in 1944, became SS Regiment 'Hungary and Austria' in 1945.
14th Waffen Grenadier Division der SS 'Galizien'	Heraldic lion	Galizien	Formed in 1943 from Ukrainians. Russia in 1944, then Slovakia. Poland, Yugoslavia then Austria in 1945.
15th Waffen Grenadier Division der SS (Lettisches No.1)	SS runes or swastika or three 5-pointed stars in ring with 11-pointed rays (fig. 28)	—	Formed in 1943 from Latvian security police. Baltic, Kurland in 1944. Prussia then Berlin in 1945.
16th SS Panzer-Grenadier Division 'Reichsführer SS'	SS runes	Reichsführer SS	Formed in 1943. Corsica in 1943. Italy 1944-45, then Hungary. Germany in 1945.
17th SS Panzer-Grenadier Division 'Götz von Berlichingen'	SS runes	Götz von Berlichingen	Formed in 1943. Normandy, Alsace, Ardennes 1944. Germany in 1945.
18th SS Freiwilligen Panzer-Grenadier Division 'Horst Wessel'	SA emblem	Horst Wessel	Formed in 1944 from young volunteers from Yugoslavia and Hungary. Normandy in 1944. Hungary and Czechoslovakia in 1945.

GERMAN ARMY, WAFFEN SS IV

Ranks from 1942 to 1945 : 1. SS runes (or divisional insignia, see 23 to 38) worn on the right collar patch. Left collar patches (first series of figures), shoulder straps (second series of figures) and arm chevrons (Nos. 18, 19 and 20 of the second series):

2 and 21. Schütze — 3 and 20. Oberschütze — 4 and 19. Sturmmann — 5 and 18. Rottenführer — 6 and 17. Unterscharführer — 7 and 16. Scharführer — 8 and 15. Oberscharführer — 9 and 14. Hauptscharführer — 10 and 13. Sturmscharführer — 11 and 12. Untersturmführer — 12 and 11. Obersturmführer — 13 and 10. Hauptsturmführer — 14 and 9. Sturmbannführer — 15 and 8. Obersturmbannführer — 16 and 7. Standartenführer — 17 and 6. Oberführer — 18 and 5. Brigadeführer and Generalmajor der SS — 19 and 4. Gruppenführer and Generalleutnant der SS — 20 and 3. Obergruppenführer and General der SS — 21 and 2. Oberstgruppenführer and Generaloberst der SS — 22 and 1. Reichsführer SS

Divisional insignia (right collar patch): 23. Totenkopf — 24. Prinz Eugen — 25. Nordland — 26. Handschar — 27. Galizien — 28. Lettisches Nr. 1 — 29. Horst Wessel — 30. Estnisches Nr. 1 — 31. Skanderbeg — 32. Maria Theresia (SS Cavalry Division) — 33. Kroatisches Nr. 2 — 34. Nederland — 35. Ungarisches Nr. 2 — 36. Russisches Nr. 1 — 37. Landstorm Nederland — 38. Dirlewanger

Rank insignia worn on camouflaged clothing: see 39 to 54. These correspond to the ranks given above from Unterscharführer to Oberstgruppenführer.

The arm of service was indicated by the colour of the piping on the shoulder straps of NCOs and other ranks, and as cloth underlays to officers' shoulder cords.

Light grey: General officers
White: Corps and Divisional Staff, Infantry and Grenadiers
Golden yellow: Cavalry and Reconnaissance troops
Lemon yellow: Signal units and War Correspondents
Pink: Tank and Anti-tank units
Dark Blue: Medical units
Black: Engineers
Red: Artillery
Light green: SS Police and Mountain units
Orange: Field Police
Orange red: Replacement Services
Crimson: Veterinary units
Wine red: Rocket troops and Legal services
Light pink: Transport and Maintenance troops
Light blue: Supply units, Administration and Technical Services
Dark green: Reserve Officers
Black and white twist: Tank Engineers
Light brown: Concentration Camp guards

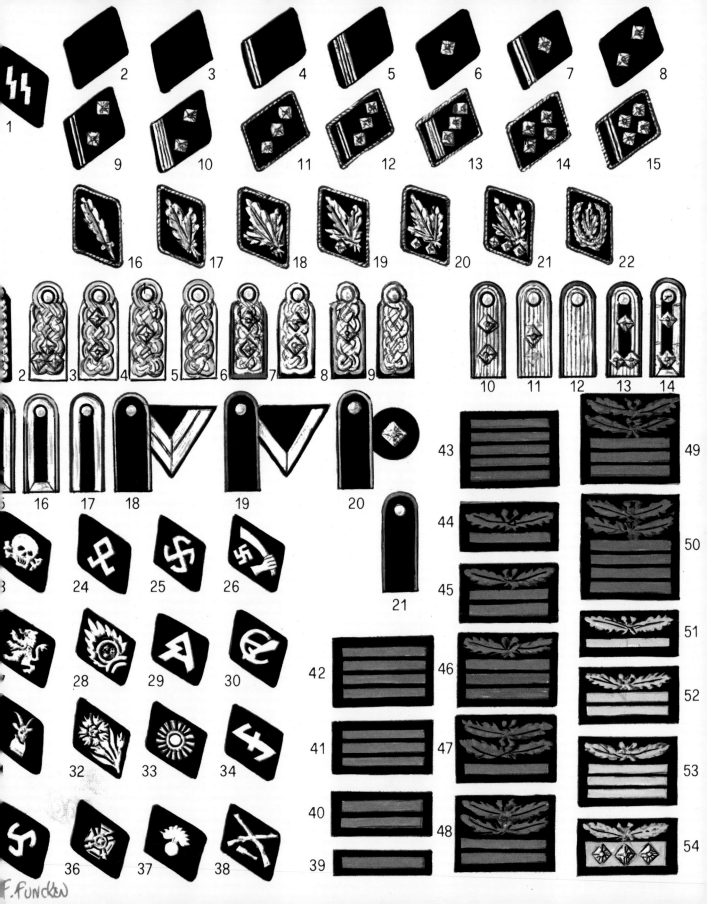

F. FUNCKEN

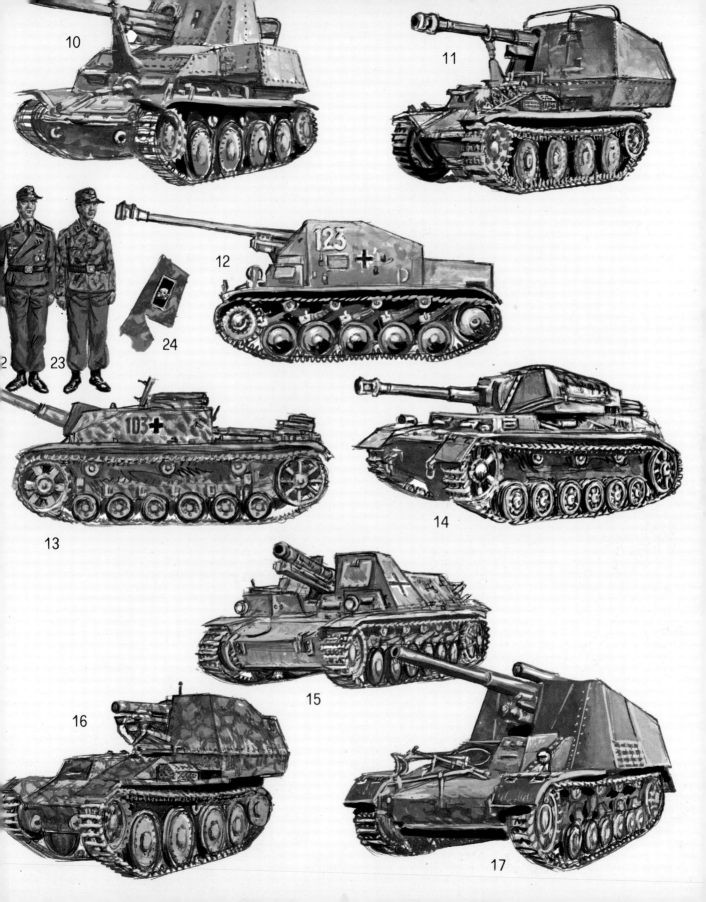

10

11

12

123

22   23

24

13   103

14

15

16

17

NUMBER AND NAME	COLLAR PATCH	CUFF TITLE	HISTORY
19th Waffen Grenadier Division der SS (Lettisches No. 2)	Double swastika	—	Formed in 1944. Russia in 1944. Kurland and Prussia in 1945.
20th Waffen Grenadier Division der SS (Estnisches No. 1)	Arm with sword and Estonian stylised E or SS runes	—	Formed in 1944 from Estonian volunteers. Baltic, Silesia then Czechoslovakia in 1945.
21st Waffen Gebirgs Division der SS 'Skanderbeg' (Albanisches No. 1)	Skanderbeg helmet	Skanderbeg	Formed in 1944 from Albanian sympathisers. Balkans, then disbanded after numerous desertions. Became 'Kampfgruppe Skanderbeg' in Yugoslavia, then on the Oder in 1945.
22nd Freiwilligen Kavallerie Division der SS 'Maria Theresia'	Cornflower with leaves and buds	—	Formed in 1944 from ethnic Germans of Hungarian nationality. Hungary, virtually annihilated at Budapest.
23rd Waffen Gebirgs Division der SS 'Kama' (Kroatisches No. 2)	Stylised sunflower		Abortive attempt at formation in 1943. Only existed from June to October 1944.
23rd Freiwilligen Panzer-Grenadier Division 'Nederland'	SS runes	Nederland General Seyffardt De Ruiter	Formed in 1943 from Dutch volunteers. Croatia then Russia in 1944. Then Estonia, Lithuania, Pomerania and finally Berlin in 1945.
24th Waffen Gebirgs 'Kartsjäger' Division der SS	SS runes	Not known	Created in 1944, apart from the battalion formed in 1943 from ethnic Germans from northern Italy. Yugoslavia and Italy from 1944 to 1945.
25th Waffen Grenadier Division der SS 'Hunyadi' (Ungarisches No. 1)	'H'	Not known	Formed in 1944. Germany in 1945. Heavy losses to the Russians, then rapid surrender to the Americans.

GERMAN ARMY, SELF-PROPELLED ARTILLERY
(pages 98-99)

1. 4·7 cm anti-tank gun on Panzer I chassis — 2. 7·62 cm Russian anti-tank gun on Panzer II chassis — 3. 7·5 cm PAK 40 anti-tank gun on a Czech 38 (t) chassis — 4. 8·8 cm PAK 43 anti-tank gun on a Panzer III/IV chassis: originally known as the 'Hornisse' (Hornet), it was re-named 'Nashorn' (Rhinoceros) in 1943 — 5. 7·5 cm assault gun (Sturmgeschütz III), 1940 — 6. 15 cm howitzer on Panzer I Model B chassis: 'Stammvater' (Ancestor) 1940 — 7. 15 cm howitzer on Czech 38 (t) chassis — 8. 10·5 cm howitzer on Panzer II Model F chassis: 'Wespe' (Wasp) — 9. 10·5 cm howitzer on Panzer III chassis: 'Sturmhaubitze' (assault howitzer) — 10. 7·62 cm Russian anti-tank gun on Czech 38 (t) chassis — 11. 7·5 cm PAK 40 anti-tank gun on Czech 38 (t) chassis — 12. 7·5 cm PAK 40 anti-tank gun on Panzer II chassis: 'Marder' (Marten) II — 13. 7·5 cm assault gun (Sturmgeschütz 40) on Panzer III chassis — 14. 10·5 cm howitzer on Panzer IVB chassis — 15. 15 cm howitzer on Panzer II chassis — 16. 15 cm howitzer on Czech 38 (t) chassis — 17. 15 cm howitzer on Panzer III/IV chassis: 'Hummel' (Bumble Bee). (The vehicles illustrated here are not all drawn to the same scale.) — 18. Collar and shoulder strap insignia worn by self-propelled gun crews attached to the infantry — 19. Collar and shoulder strap insignia of a Fähnrich serving with the self-propelled artillery attached to armoured units — 20–21. Field-grey uniform worn by self-propelled gun crews: Other ranks (left) and Officer (right) — 22. Panzerjäger or member of a tank destroyer crew — 23–24. Panzerjäger with camouflaged jacket and detail of collar insignia. The death's head emblem indicates that the wearer belongs to an armoured unit and not to the Waffen SS.

GERMAN ARMY, SELF-PROPELLED GUNS ON FRENCH CHASSIS

1. 7·5 cm anti-tank gun on Lorraine chassis — 2. 10·5 cm howitzer on Lorraine chassis — 3. 15 cm howitzer on Lorraine chassis — 4. 4·7 cm anti-tank gun on Lorraine chassis — 5. 7·5 cm PAK 40 anti-tank gun on Hotchkiss chassis — 6. 10·5 cm howitzer on Hotchkiss H 39 chassis — 7. 4·7 cm anti-tank gun on Renault R 35 chassis — 8. 3·7 cm anti-tank gun on Renault Chenillette infantry carrier chassis — 9. 10·5 cm howitzer on FCM tank chassis — 10. 7·5 cm PAK 40 anti-tank gun on FCM tank chassis

1

2

3

4

5

6

7

8

9

10

NUMBER AND NAME	COLLAR PATCH	CUFF TITLE	HISTORY
26th Waffen Grenadier Division der SS (Ungarisches No. 2)	Not known	Not known	Formed in 1944 but only on paper. Its elements disappeared in Normandy.
27th SS Freiwilligen Grenadier Division 'Langemarck'	Three-armed swastika	Langemarck	Formed in 1943 from Flemish volunteers of the Flemish Legion created in Belgium in 1940. Russia from 1943 to 1944. Germany in 1945.
28th SS Freiwilligen Panzer-Grenadier Division 'Wallonie'	SS runes	Wallonien	Formed in 1943 from Walloon volunteers of the Walloon Legion created in Belgium in 1940. Russia in 1943 to 1944, then Ardennes and Germany from 1944 to 1945.
29th Waffen Grenadier Division der SS (Russisches No. 1), also called 'Kaminski'	Maltese cross with swords	—	Formed in 1944. Disbanded after the sacking of Warsaw and the execution of its commander by the SS, after complaints by General Guderian, who had been appalled by its excesses.
29th Waffen Grenadier Division der SS (Italienisches No. 1)	SS runes or 'fasces'	—	Formed in Italy in 1944. Only received the vacant number of the above formation in 1945. Surrendered the following month.
30th Waffen Grenadier Division der SS (Russisches No. 2)	Trident of St. Vladimir, or Eastern Orthodox Church Cross, or wolf's head, or shield and sword	—	Formed in 1944. France then Germany from 1944 to 1945.
31st SS Freiwilligen Grenadier Division	Not known	Not known	Formed on paper in 1944. Never existed as a division. Germany in 1945.
32nd SS Freiwilligen Panzer-Grenadier Division '30. Januar'	SS runes	30. Januar	Formed in 1945. Russia, then defence of Berlin.
33rd Waffen Kavallerie Division der SS (Ungarisches No. 3)	Sword and oak leaves	—	Formed in 1944-45 in Hungary. Decimated in Hungary then incorporated into the division mentioned below.
33rd Waffen Grenadier Division der SS 'Charlemagne' (Französisches No. 1)	SS runes	Charlemagne	Formed partly from the Legion of French volunteers in 1944. Russia, then Germany and defence of Berlin in 1945.
34th Waffen Grenadier Division der SS 'Landstorm Nederland'	SS runes or grenade with flame or Dutch Nazi Party symbol	Landstorm Nederland	Formed in Holland in 1944. Holland then Germany in 1945.
35th SS Polizei Grenadier Division	SS runes	Not known	Formed in 1944. Germany from 1944 to 1945.
36th SS Sturm-Division 'Dirlewanger'	Crossed rifles with grenade	—	Formed in 1945, partly from 'special battalions' of convicts and commanded by Dr Oskar Dirlewanger. Germany.
37th SS Freiwilligen Kavallerie Division 'Lützow'	SS runes	Not known	Formed in 1945 partly from the remnants of two SS cavalry divisions. Austria.
38th SS Panzer-Grenadier Division 'Nibelungen'	Not known	Not known	Formed in 1945 from staff and students of SS officers' schools and Himmler's guards. Brief active service in Germany.

GERMAN ARMOURED VEHICLES I

1. Panzer II 'Luchs' (Lynx) — 2. Panzer III Model L — 3. Panzer III Model M — 4. Panzer IV Model G — 5. Black Panzer beret (Schutzmütze) worn by Wehrmacht (left) and SS Panzer troops — 6. Black field service cap (Feldmütze) worn by Wehrmacht (left) and SS Panzer troops — 7. Black general issue field cap (Einheitsfeldmütze) worn by Wehrmacht (left) and SS Panzer Troops — 8. Standard steel helmet worn by Wehrmacht tank crews

Self-propelled guns

Designed to support the infantry by accompanying the assault waves, the Wehrmacht's first self-propelled guns numbered only six when they took part in the operations involved in the Battle of France. They bore the designation *Sturmgeschütz* (assault gun) III, and looked like tanks with extra-low silhouettes; this design was very advanced for the period, foreshadowing as it did the modern tank destroyers which were only to appear four years later. Although it immediately became apparent that they could perform a very useful service, these half-dozen monsters nevertheless tended to be forgotten, and their production was severely curbed as the production of battle tanks became more urgent. These had performed wonders throughout the years 1939 and 1940, and their numbers now had to be increased rapidly in preparation for the imminent attack on the Soviet Union.

The *Sturmgeschütz* III, then, was an assault gun attached to the artillery and designed to fire shells from its short-barrelled 75 mm gun almost point-blank at the variety of obstacles which the infantry might encounter in the course of an attack. The first Model A was followed, in 1941 and 1942, by the B, C, D and E versions, which differed very little in their general appearance from the first *Sturmgeschütz*.

At this stage in the war the unpleasant surprise of the new generation of Russian tanks caused the Germans to realise the urgent need for more powerful anti-tank weapons. They responded by considerably improving their self-propelled artillery, creating the *Sturmgeschütz* 40 Model F, which was better armed and better protected. Henceforth the main role of this assault gun was the destruction of enemy tanks which were attacking the infantry. Because it was itself vulnerable to attacks from enemy infantry, it had to be provided with a weapon suitable for this type of close combat, and the excellent MG34 or MG42 machine gun was chosen for this purpose.

To help the infantry in their attacks on fortified positions, the *Sturmhaubitze* armed with a 10·5 cm howitzer was produced at the rate of three hundred a year; this figure, however, was still relatively small in comparison with the production figures for the other models: 778 in 1942, 3,000 in 1943 and 4,800 in 1944. These pieces of equipment also saw service within the armoured divisions themselves; in these cases the crews wore the traditional black tanker's uniform, while the crews of the self-propelled assault guns attached to the infantry wore a special uniform of similar design but in field-grey *(feldgrau)*.[1]

PANZERARTILLERIE AND GESCHÜTZWAGEN[2]

Besides the *Sturmgeschütz*, the standard and specially-designed assault gun, a large family of hybrids, based on the chassis of light German and Czech tanks, was developed from 1939 onwards. However, the fighting on the Eastern Front in 1941 clearly revealed their disturbing inadequacy in armour and weapons. Driven on by sheer necessity, the Germans improvised an enormous number of more powerful vehicles, generally by mounting a gun of the appropriate calibre on the chassis of tanks collected from wherever they could be found, but particularly from France. The resulting vehicles all too often looked frighteningly clumsy, and it is a fact that many of these machines were quite unsuitable for the poor Russian roads. Also, the weight of the gun often damaged the suspension of the tanks' chassis which were too light for the purpose. This was the case with the 15 cm howitzer on the Panzer I chassis, known as the *Stammvater* (literally 'Ancestor'), and also with the 37 mm anti-tank guns mounted on French Lorraine troop carriers *(chenillettes)* or British Bren carriers.

1 The new field-grey uniform, of identical cut to that of the tankers, was later adopted by anti-tank crews attached to the armoured divisions, for their original black dress was too easily spotted from a distance when they left their vehicles to locate the enemy.
2 Armoured artillery and self-propelled guns (more or less improvised).

GERMAN ARMOURED VEHICLES II

1. Panther Model D — 2. Panther Model A — 3. Tiger I Model E — 4. Tank crew member in standard army greatcoat — 5. Tank crew member in traditional black Panzer uniform — 6. Waffen SS tank crew member. Note the position of the national emblem on the field service cap and arm.

1

2

4

5

6

3

·P.F.Funcken

On the other hand, the self-propelled anti-tank gun produced in 1939, which was armed with a Czech 47 mm gun and was known as the *Panzerjäger* I, performed well against British armoured vehicles right from the beginning of the North Africa Campaign. Its 'big brother', the *Panzerjäger* 38, with its Russian 76·2 mm gun mounted on a Czech chassis, inflicted heavy losses on enemy tanks up to 1942. This type of tank destroyer was continually improved, and constituted the backbone of the self-propelled anti-tank equipment of the German army until models appeared which were better adapted to current operational conditions.

The many models which were produced almost simultaneously in 1942 had a common feature which placed them at a disadvantage in comparison with the standard *Sturmgeschütz*: this lay in the poor protection given to the crew, who had to fight in a three-sided open-topped turret without rear armour, thereby placing them at the mercy of the smallest grenade thrown with any degree of accuracy. For this reason, these vehicles always fought under the protection of the infantry.

The models which appeared subsequently, from 1943 onwards, were real monsters, bulky in appearance and with formidable armament and armour protection in the anti-tank as well as in the assault gun versions. It must be noted, however, that although they were easier to produce than tanks, the self-propelled guns suffered from a major drawback, namely that the guns themselves had only a limited traverse, while the heavier the models became the less easy they were to manoeuvre.

The growth of enemy air power, coupled with the increasing weakness of the Luftwaffe, led inevitably to the development of armoured anti-aircraft vehicles, whose evolution will be described in volume 4, in the chapter on anti-aircraft guns.

The German industrialists tirelessly pursued their design and development studies right up to the last months of the war. The reader will also see the outcome of their final discoveries in volume 4.

German Armoured Vehicles 1941 to 1943

From the creation of the armoured force in 1934 until 1943 German tank designers never strayed far from the conventional lines of the *Panzerkampfwagen* I, II, III and IV, which had played such a magnificent part in the victorious *Blitzkrieg* campaigns. However, during the years 1941 to 1943, and particularly after the first experiences on the Russian Front, a very marked change took place in the area of armour and weapons now that the outmoded concepts of the 'lightning war' were becoming less and less appropriate.

The first clashes with the Soviet heavy tanks had quickly demonstrated the relative impotence of the German tanks' guns, as well as the inadequacy of their armour, which could not withstand the onslaught of the T34s armed with their formidable 76·2 mm guns. The anti-tank artillery, too, originally limited to 37 mm and even smaller calibre weapons, such as the 25 mm gun used in France, found itself completely outclassed and had to be considerably developed in the face of this new threat. It was recalled that in 1917 Ludendorff had employed all available field artillery of all calibres to stop the Allied tanks, and this strategy was now revived.

Apart from Germany, which had clung to this principle since the end of the First World War, all the other belligerents had applied themselves to the task of creating specialised anti-tank weapons which, in the end, only demonstrated the truth of what a few had claimed in vain all along: namely, that the destructive power of small calibre weapons on light armour plating had been overestimated.[1] During the first two years of the war, then, the calibre of anti-tank

1 See vol. 1.

GERMAN ARMOURED VEHICLES III

1. Panzer II AB — 2. Saurer (Austrian) armoured artillery observation vehicle — 3. Panzer III Type F6 and H — 4. Panzer III 'Special' — 5. Afrika Korps tank crew members wearing tropical uniforms. The death's head emblems are worn on the lapels of the jacket.

1

2

3

5   6

4

X.F.Funcken

weapons used by front-line troops underwent a rapid increase without parallel in the history of warfare. In addition, the muzzle velocity of projectiles increased far beyond what had previously been considered adequate. The fact that the thickness of armour plate never kept pace with this increase in calibre of the new weapons is a remarkable illustration of how little understood was the defensive potential of armour plating.

It must also be emphasised that the armour plate could be thickened on the new generation of heavy tanks in proportion to the increase in tonnage; indeed, the fact that the armour alone accounted for only a fraction of the total weight meant that the vital parts of the tank could now be more effectively protected; henceforth, the surface area of such tanks did not increase as rapidly as their volume and weight, as had been the case with the last heavily manned monsters which had failed so lamentably against the Germans in France and Russia.

The first models of the Panzer I and II, which were too light and inadequately armed, were now to be relegated to less ambitious roles. They finally disappeared from the ranks of the Panzer divisions in 1943. Fifteen hundred units of the Panzer I were built up to 1939, but production of this model had ceased by 1941. Henceforth they were used for training and for infantry support duties or, as happened to some three hundred and fifty of them, converted into self-propelled anti-tank guns. A command tank version also played a significant role to the rear of the powerful armoured divisions.

The Panzer IIs had been the main equipment of the Panzer divisions between 1939 and 1942, but after 1943 these too were generally turned into self-propelled guns. An interesting, lighter variant called the *Luchs* (Lynx) served as a reconnaissance tank and was produced up to 1943. Widely used on the Russian Front, the Lynx could reach 60 km/h but its thin armour and comparatively feeble armament (one 20 mm cannon and one 7·9 mm machine gun) led to its speedy withdrawal from front-line duties.

At the outbreak of war there were ninety-eight Panzer IIIs and two hundred and eleven Panzer IVs in the Panzer divisions. Their production was stepped up considerably in the light of the decision to launch

'Operation Barbarossa' against Russia in June 1941, and by that date there were four hundred and forty Panzer IIIs and five hundred and seventeen Panzer IVs in service.

We saw in the first volume of this work how the Germans, by their skill in manoeuvres, had managed to defeat the masses of Soviet tanks until the Russians' entirely new armoured fighting vehicle, the T34, arrived on the scene. Only supply difficulties, due to the fact that the factories producing the T34 were located in Siberia, prevented this seemingly indestructible adversary from being used on a massive scale before the beginning of 1942, but General Guderian was only too aware of the mortal threat which this new tank posed.

In fact the introduction of the T34 caused immense repercussions throughout the belligerents' armed forces, immediately bringing pressure to bear on those responsible for German arms production to initiate a new development programme to produce a successor to the Panzer IV; the need for such a project had been largely overlooked in the succession of easy victories achieved up to this point. The officers at the front, practical soldiers that they were, clamoured merely for a straightforward copy of the T34, but the technicians at home, fussing over points of detail and subject too to Hitler's bullying, sought to improve on the captured tanks and produced for the Führer their own plans for what were virtually land fortresses weighing nearly a hundred tons. This shilly-shallying, and the fact that design studies were feverishly conducted on several prototypes at the same time, in the end only delayed the appearance of the much-needed tank.

In the meantime, while every inch of ground was being bitterly contested, the German tanks at the front were being protected by the best means available, thanks to improvised methods such as the strengthening of frontal armour with layers of spare track lengths. The year 1942 was to see the biggest

GERMAN ARMOURED VEHICLES IV

1. Panzer IV Model E with the insignia of the Afrika Korps — 2. Panzer IV Model F2 — 3. Panzer VI Tiger Model E — 4–5. Afrika Korps tank crew members in greatcoat (left) and the standard Tropical dress (right) worn at the beginning of the campaign in North Africa

1

2

3

4   5

A.F. Funcken

production of the Panzer II Model M, with its reinforced turret armour, nineteen hundred of which were built.

Guns were increased in calibre, from the 37 mm to the long-barrelled 50 mm gun for the Panzer III, and from the short-barrelled 75 mm to the long-barrelled 75 mm gun in the case of the Panzer IV. These new guns had much greater penetrating power, for the velocity of their shells was now in the region of 750 metres per second. Self-propelled guns, too, originally designed to support the forward elements of the Panzer divisions, were increased to the maximum possible number in an attempt to stem the waves of heavy Soviet tanks. As has been seen in the previous chapter, sheer necessity even led to the use of French and Czech tank chassis for this purpose.

Meanwhile the Panzer IV had been fitted with armoured skirts, which protected its sides by causing anti-tank shells to explode before they reached the tank's main armour or tracks. These side skirts were made of steel mesh on the Model J, of which eight hundred and fifty examples were produced, and these remained in service right up to the end of the war. In addition the Panzer IV was equipped with a special type of wide track known as an *Ostkette* (or literally 'eastern chain'), which enabled it to move about more efficiently in the Russian snows and quagmires. It can be asserted that the Panzer IV remained the main trump card of the German armoured divisions throughout the war, in spite of the fact that it was not the best tank that Germany possessed. Eight thousand of them were manufactured in all.

'PANTHERS' AND 'TIGERS'

It was the firms of Henschel, Porsche, Daimler-Benz and Mann who were given the task of producing rival design prototypes of those new tanks which came to bear the names of the big cats. Both Daimler-Benz and Mann were in a position to unveil their prototypes as early as March 1942. Although the model produced by Mann was adopted initially, it was later cancelled, to be replaced by the Daimler-Benz design, with its 75 mm gun which was twice the length of that fitted to the Panzer IV. The new tank, designated the Panzer V

and called the 'Panther' (a name which was only officially granted to it in February 1944), was the first weapon capable of meeting the Soviet T34 on anything like an equal footing. This new German medium tank began to appear on the battlefield in the middle of 1943 and it soon established itself as one of the best tanks of the Second World War. Its production was eventually to reach a total of nearly six thousand units.

Curiously the first model was the Panther D. The Panther A version followed, the only apparent difference between the two being a machine gun fitted to the latter for close-quarter defence. Then came the third and last version, the Panther G.

In April 1942, a month after the appearance of the Panther prototypes, the firms of Henschel and Porsche submitted their own designs for rigorous examination by the army's technical branches. The Henschel design was adopted, but it was subjected to many modifications and personal counter-orders from the Führer before it could be put into production. The new tank, the *Panzerkampfwagen* VI, was christened the Tiger Model E, then, more simply, the Tiger I; it bore some resemblance to an earlier model planned in 1937 and bearing the designation *Durchbruchswagen* (breakthrough tank).

The Tiger had been provided with a formidable 88 mm gun, a modified version, mounted in a tank turret, of the famous 88 mm anti-aircraft gun, whose effectiveness against tanks had been demonstrated by Rommel in North Africa. The gun gave the tank an easily recognisable silhouette, its long barrel measuring more than half the total length of the vehicle. Like those of the Panther, the tracks of the Tiger rode on interleaved road wheels, a special feature which also offered additional protection. Its armour was the thickest ever produced, at the front of the turret reaching the almost impenetrable thickness of 102 mm. By aiming at the sides of the turret, where the armour was only 62 mm thick, the 76·2 mm guns

GERMAN ARMOURED VEHICLES V

1. Sd.Kfz.250/10 half-track armoured reconnaissance vehicle with 3·7 cm anti-tank gun — 2. Triple 2 cm anti-aircraft machine gun mounting on Sd.Kfz. 251 semi-tracked personnel carrier — 3. Sd.Kfz. 234/3 armoured car — 4. Sd.Kfz. 234/2 'Puma' armoured car

1

2

3

4

F.Funcken

SYNOPSIS OF THE PRINCIPAL GERMAN TANKS[1]

TYPE	WEIGHT	SPEED	OPERATIONAL RANGE (WITHOUT RE-FUELLING)	ARMAMENT	CREW	INTRODUCED INTO SERVICE
Panzerspähwagen 'Luchs' (Lynx), the reconnaissance version of the Panzerkampfwagen II L	11.8 tons	60 km/h	250 km	One 20 mm gun	3 or 4	1941
Pz. Kpfw. III L and M	22.3 tons	45 km/h	135 km	One long 5 cm gun Two 7·9 mm machine guns	5	1942
Pz. Kpfw. III N	22.3 tons	45 km/h	135 km	One short 7·5 cm gun Two 7·9 mm machine guns	5	1943
Pz. Kpfw. IV F	23.6 tons	37 km/h	200 km	One long 7·5 cm gun Two 7·9 mm machine guns	5	1942
Pz. Kpfw. IV G	23.5 tons	38 km/h	200 km	One long 7·5 cm gun Two 7·9 mm machine guns	5	1942
Pz. Kpfw. IV J	25 tons	38 km/h	300 km	One long 7·5 cm gun Two 7·9 mm machine guns	5	1943
Pz. Kpfw. V 'Panther D'	43 tons	46 km/h	200 km	One long 7·5 cm gun Two 7·9 mm machine guns	4	1943
Pz. Kpfw. V 'Panther G'	44.8 tons	46 km/h	200 km	One long 7·5 cm gun Two 7·9 mm machine guns	4	1943
Pz. Kpfw. VI 'Tiger' Model E or 'Tiger I'	55 tons	37 km/h	100 km	One long 88 mm gun Two 7·9 mm machine guns	5	1942

1 See the table on page 120 of volume 1 for the older tanks.

of the Soviet T34 and KV tanks managed to knock out many Tigers, but first they had to take considerable risks to get close enough.

The first thirteen Tiger Is were delivered in 1942 and a production rate of over twenty-five examples a month resulted in the end in some 1,350[1] units being built.

Nor was Dr Porsche's prototype completely forgotten; Henschel's unlucky rival was given the opportunity of applying his ideas to the production of an 88 mm self-propelled gun which was called the 'Ferdinand', the Christian name of the inventor of the Volkswagen. Later on it became known as the 'Elephant'. This vehicle was classed as a tank destroyer.[2]

Meanwhile, the Soviet threat had made the need for an increase in tank production more urgent. In 1942 4,278 tanks emerged from the factories and 5,966 were built in 1943, figures which were to be surpassed in 1944. In the first half of that year some 5,500 were made, a rate of production which was somehow or other maintained until May 1945.

1 The Tiger II, or Royal Tiger is described in vol. 4.

2 These vehicles are discussed in vol. 4.

ARMOURED CARS

Although produced on a relatively modest scale compared with tanks and self-propelled guns, armoured cars nevertheless played an important role throughout the war. It is a curious fact that although the Germans never ceased to equip their tanks with bigger guns than those of the enemy, they allowed themselves to be outclassed in the field of armoured cars. As they apparently relied upon their speed and mobility, they were anxious not to weigh them down with more powerful weapons or thicker armour, although they did make exceptions on some later models which we shall mention further on.

The armoured cars were divided into two main types: a light four-wheeled type and a heavy eight-wheeled type. A third, six-wheeled type, which was manufactured up to the outbreak of war, only played a limited part in the campaigns in Poland and France. This was a transitional type which helped to support the lighter vehicles until the heavy eight-wheelers were introduced.

The Four-Wheelers

The very first model, the Kfz13,[1] created in 1934, appears to have played a very brief part in the opening battles. It was used in Poland in infantry reconnaissance sections. The three other main four-wheeled types were the Sd.Kfz or *Sonderkraftfahrzeuge* (literally 'special cars') Nos 221, 222 and 223. The 222 was by far the most widely distributed, differing from the 221 in that it had a cannon instead of a machine gun. The 223 was fitted with complete radio equipment.

The Six-Wheelers

There were three types of six-wheelers: the Sd.Kfz 231, with a 20 mm gun and a machine gun, the 232 with the same armament and a radio, and the 263 with a machine gun and radio.

The Eight-Wheelers

The three heavy eight-wheeled models bore the same designations as their predecessors when they replaced them at the front. Whereas the six-wheelers had a top speed of 70 km/h, and the four-wheelers nearly 80 km/h, the eight-wheelers could reach 100 km/h. In 1944 they were superseded by the new generation of 'Puma' Series 234 armoured cars which, for the first time, were given the powerful armament of, initially, a 50 mm gun and, later, a 75 mm gun.

Half-tracks

Numerous types of armoured half-tracks appeared even before the war. They will be found in the chapter on The Motorised Army in vol. 3.

1 See the illustrations on page 115 of vol. 1.

The Luftwaffe from 1941 to 1943

After his crushing victory on the Continent, Hitler hurled his Luftwaffe into the attack on the British Isles, which now alone remained to take up the challenge. The enthusiasm of the German pilots was enormous. They spoke of themselves as being 'harder than Krupp steel' and sang, like the professional chorus of an opera, a new and highly successful military march: '... *und wir fahren gegen Engeland*' (... and we are marching against England).

The German airmen, however, could muster up no real hate for their last remaining opponent, and like the vast majority of their compatriots they regretted that they now had to crush the arrogant 'Albion' to force upon it the defeat which already seemed inevitable. The Nazi propagandists were only too well aware of such feelings and the most fantastic reports were made about the panic which reigned throughout Britain in anticipation of the terrible retribution which awaited her. It was claimed that the British people had taken to drink to bolster up their flagging courage, and that British Jews were besieging the cosmetic surgery clinics to have their noses altered.

In reality, as we have seen in the chapter on the British army, this was entirely untrue. But, more important, the Luftwaffe found itself quite incapable of effecting alone what it had previously achieved with the cooperation of the formidable formations of the Wehrmacht. The fighters, although excellent in some respects, had insufficient range to sustain long aerial combats over Britain, and as a result they were even less capable of protecting the bomber squadrons, whose task it was to wipe out the key industrial centres spread over the United Kingdom. The Home Fleet, ready to smash the amphibious assault waves, was in itself an extremely difficult obstacle to overcome, even with the help of submarines, of which in any case there were still far too few.

Mastery of the air, which was indispensable to the success of Operation Sealion, was in fact never to be secured, despite the confidence of the leaders of the Third Reich. And in fact, although they did not dare to admit it, many highly placed German generals and admirals were taking a considerably more realistic view and had no illusions as to the likely outcome of the ambitious plan.

The RAF, and Fighter Command in particular, were to show that this pessimism was justified, but not without paying the shockingly high price of 449 pilots killed between 10 July and 31 October 1940.

THE MESSERSCHMITT ME. 109

This exceptional fighter, whose early development was described in the first part of this volume, still formed the backbone of the German fighter arm. It was to continue in this role throughout the war, in spite of the new and improved types which appeared in the course of the following years.

In July 1940 there were some eight hundred Me. 109s, and by the following month the German fighter arm was able to deploy 935 of these planes, just in time for the great battles of the *Adlerangriff* (Attack of the Eagle) and the bloody *Adlertag* or 'Eagle Day' of 13 August.

LUFTWAFFE I
THE MESSERSCHMITT Me.109

Defence of the Reich: 1 and 2. Me.109G — 3. Me.109 F.
Africa: 4, 5 and 6
Russian Front: 7 to 10. Fig. 7 shows an Me.109 G 'Gustav' with two 21 cm WGr.21 'Dodel' rocket-launching tubes, used from 1942 onwards.
All these aircraft show the distinctive camouflage and marking schemes which were used by the Luftwaffe from the middle of the war until the end of hostilities. Many other schemes existed which combined colours and markings in an ingenious way.

The Me.109E variant, which was the chief plane of the fighter units, had an armoured windshield like those of its opponents, the Hurricane and Spitfire. Its armament comprised two 20 mm cannon in the wings, each firing sixty rounds, and two 7·9 mm machine guns in the engine cowling firing two thousand rounds, or alternatively two 7·9 mm machine guns firing five thousand rounds and one 20 mm cannon firing through the propeller boss, with a stock of 180 shells.

Confident of victory, the pilots hurled themselves into the fight to sweep the opposing and numerically inferior fighter force from the sky. Some of them, ironically, had written on their fuselage: 'London 15 August. Finished!' British tenacity, which even the Germans recognised and sportingly acknowledged, would be put to a stiff test, particularly on 15 August, when almost the whole of the Luftwaffe was flung into the battle. Between 8 and 18 August the RAF Fighter Command lost 183 machines and 94 pilots, but still they managed to hold on by calling on young airmen, many with only a few flying hours to their credit. At the conclusion of the offensive, the Luftwaffe had lost six hundred and ten Me.109Es, of which some 10 per cent had plunged into the Channel when they ran out of fuel. On the other hand, the Messerschmitts claimed most of the British aircraft destroyed: one hundred and seventy machines of all types.

After this terrible struggle, an improved Me.109 was introduced, the F1 version, which had a superior operational ceiling to the Spitfire and which began service in 1941. The F2 which followed differed from the F1 only in its modified armament. A 'tropical' version was also produced to support Rommel's forces in North Africa.

Then in 1942 came the F3 model, followed by the F4 and F5 versions, which again differed mainly in their armaments. A much more outstanding model was the Me.109G, of which 6,500 examples were built in 1943 alone, whereas only 2,600 of the E and F variants had been produced in 1941. Christened 'Gustav' by the pilots, the new variant had one 20 mm cannon and two 13 mm machine guns. The prominent breeches of these machine guns were betrayed by two protuberances on the engine cowling, features which earned the 'Gustav' the nickname 'Beule' (hump).

THE FOCKE-WULF Fw. 190

The dazzling successes achieved by the Messerschmitt Me.109 on all fronts did not prevent the Germans from designing and producing another fighter, whose prototypes had been flying for some time. The Focke-Wulf was to win an equally glorious reputation and nearly fourteen thousand units were produced.[1] The new fighter, powerfully armed, outclassed the Spitfire Mk IX by virtue of its doubly superior firepower, and its appearance in the bloody struggle gave the Luftwaffe an undoubted ascendancy during the summer of 1941.

Design studies for this splendid aircraft had been begun in 1937, to give the Luftwaffe a second string to its bow. The main feature of the first model to enter service was a radial engine which gave it a top speed of 768 km/h. Its phenomenal manoeuvrability at high altitude, its ability to perform breathtaking nose-dives, and its powers of acceleration, all made it a particularly tough opponent in the hands of an experienced pilot.

There were several versions of the Focke-Wulf, which again differed mainly in their armament, and which ranged from the A1 to the A10 version. A new model, the 'long-nosed' Fw.190, appeared in 1943.[2]

1 Excluding 6,700 of fighter-bomber version.
2 See vol. 4.

THE STUKA AND ITS EVOLUTION

The Junkers Ju.87 had performed its impressive dives throughout the campaigns in Poland, Belgium and France in skies which were virtually clear of enemy aircraft, but no doubts had yet been cast on its likely effectiveness in future operations. In the course of July 1940 two hundred and fifty Ju.87s of the *Stukagruppen* were finally ready for the attack on the British Isles. The first sorties were aimed at coastal shipping traffic, but it was August before these aircraft, with their predatory silhouettes, embarked on their first mass attacks on Britain.

The results were soon found to be catastrophic. Singled out by the British fighters, even when they were escorted by Me.109s, the Stukas suffered severe losses which, as the days went by, were to become progressively heavier, and the slaughter soon reached such a level that on 30 August the Luftwaffe High Command was forced to withdraw its dive-bombers from the battle. The reason for this setback was simple: the Stuka was slow, and its top speed of 385 km/h made it an easy victim for a fast fighter. Moreover, its relatively weak armament was limited to a single rearward-firing 7·9 mm machine gun and two machine guns of the same calibre in the wings.

During 1940 these weaknesses were to some extent rectified, the Ju.87D model benefiting from improvements to the aerodynamics, armament, armour and power plant. This Ju.87D was produced in successively improved versions—from the D1 to the D8 variant—and, with more and more powerful armament, was mainly employed on the Russian Front. However, the increasing aggressiveness of the new Soviet fighters made its operations more dangerous than ever. Nevertheless, the Stuka remained, in spite of all these factors, because of the difficulty of finding a feasible way to create a suitable replacement. Production even increased again in 1943, before coming to a final halt in 1944. It is estimated that, in all, some five thousand Stukas were built.

The last model, the Ju. 87G, produced in 1942, was the *Panzerknacker or* 'tank-busting' Stuka. It was armed with two 37 mm Flak 18 cannon and was a formidable weapon in the hands of skilled pilots, the most famous of whom was Hans Ulrich Rudel, a death-defying pilot who carried out some 2,350 combat missions and destroyed more than five hundred Soviet tanks.

Such extraordinary and in fact unique performances in the history of air warfare may lead one to believe that the aircraft had been markedly improved, but it was due much more to the prodigious skill and steely nerves of the German airman that these results were achieved, and then only because he took unparalleled risks and indulged in breathtaking games of hide-and-seek with the Soviet fighters.

LUFTWAFFE III

1. Henschel 126 — 2. Henschel 129 — 3. Junkers Ju.87 'Stuka' in Africa — 4. 'Stuka' G1 with 37 mm Flak 18 anti-tank cannon — 5. 'Stuka' in Russia — 6. Focke-Wulf Fw.200 G3 'Condor'. Its radius of action of nearly 2,175 miles enabled it to locate Allied convoys and report their position to U-boats. — 7. Focke-Wulf 189 (reconnaissance aircraft) — 8. Fieseler 'Storch' (Stork). Over 2,500 examples of this versatile reconnaissance and observation aircraft were built.

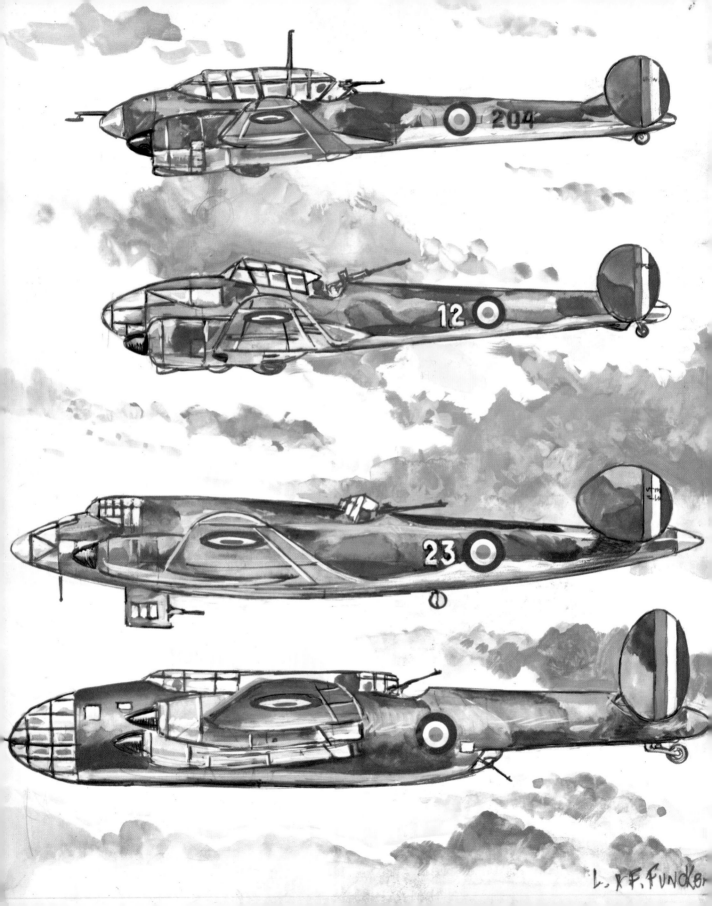

L. & F. Funcken